PRAISE FOR
X-RAY OF THE PRIEST
IN A FIELD HOSPITAL

This call 'back to basics' for the Latin clergy, set within a clear doctrinal framework, is written with both imagination and rigour, and merits a wide readership, including bishops and religious superiors.

— FR AIDAN NICHOLS, OP, author of *Holy Order: The Apostolic Ministry from the New Testament to the Second Vatican Council*

No priest doing his duty, trying to love God and neighbor, and trying to pick up his daily cross will suddenly decide, "I think I'll have a go at some adultery." He might wind up in grave treason to Our Lord, but the winding will not be sudden. He will slide into it. Conversely, he will not be able to jump up to the heights of sanctity; he'll have to climb. This book will be of great value to anyone who would like to know how to avoid the slide, and what to do in order to climb. Fr. de Malleray's timely yet classic approach to the priesthood in our times is a jewel. I thank God he wrote it.

—FR JAMES JACKSON, FSSP, author of *Nothing Superfluous*

This book presents a convincing and compelling account of the stamp and character of the priest. It is at once profoundly practical and sublimely spiritual. We have over forty men in our Faculty preparing for lives as priests across China, Latin America, East and South East Asia. I am convinced that every single one of them will profit greatly and be strengthened in their vocations by reading and re-reading carefully, attentively and prayerfully Fr de Malleray's advice.

—REVD PROF STEPHEN MORGAN, Rector of the University of Saint Joseph, Macao, China

Written from an unapologetically traditionalist position, this book is in no way less spiritually challenging and thought provoking. One does not have to agree with everything in it to come away with much material to help one discern how to be a better priest in the contemporary Church. There is also a good section on vocations.

—REVD DR MICHAEL CULLINAN MA(OXON), MA St (Cantab), PhD (Cantab), STD (Alfonsianum), Director of Maryvale Higher Institute of Religious Sciences

Fr de Malleray's reflections on the nature of the priesthood are fascinating and perceptive, and will edify both clerical and lay readers.

— DR JOSEPH SHAW, PhD, Oxf, Chairman of *The Latin Mass Society*

Father de Malleray has once more strengthened the *sensus fidei*, refining the themes introduced in *Ego Eimi* to focus more particularly on the gift of the Sacred Priesthood. We are grateful to Father for having penned these reflections, covering a wide variety of aspects about the greatest dignity conferred on man. His words gained particular resonance among our Sisters, who are dedicated to prayer, sacrifice and hospitality toward priests, as well as the making of sacred vestments. May Father's meditations encourage an even deeper urgency in spiritual support of our priests, that they may ever remain faithful to their own vocations, and in handing down the traditions and fullness of our holy faith. This is wonderful book that I heartily recommend.

— MOTHER ABBESS CECILIA, OSB, Abbey of Our Lady of Ephesus (Benedictines of Mary, Queen of Apostles, Gower, MO)

Full of instruction yet easy to read; an inspiring *vademecum* for priests, seminarians and those considering a priestly vocation.

— FR THOMAS CREAN, OP, author of *The Mass and the Saints*

X-ray of the Priest
in a Field Hospital

X-ray of the Priest
in a Field Hospital

REFLECTIONS ON THE
SACRED PRIESTHOOD

FR ARMAND DE MALLERAY, FSSP

AROUCA
PRESS

Imprimi Potest:
Very Rev Andrzej Komorowski, FSSP, Superior General
Fribourg, Switzerland, 6th February 2020

Nihil Obstat:
Very Rev Mgr Peter Fleetwood, *Censor Deputatus*
Liverpool, United Kingdom, 8th May 2020

Imprimatur:
✠ Most Rev Malcolm McMahon OP, Archbishop of Liverpool
Liverpool, England, 11th May 2020

The author thanks the various priests and laity who generously gave
time to proof-read the book and suggest valuable modifications.

ISBN: 978-1-989905-01-2 (pbk)
ISBN: 978-1-989905-02-9 (hardcover)

Arouca Press
PO Box 55003
Bridgeport PO
Waterloo, ON N2J3G0
Canada
www.aroucapress.com
Send inquiries to info@aroucapress.com

Book and cover design by
Michael Schrauzer

TABLE OF CONTENTS

PREFACE xi

1 THE FOURTEEN STATIONS OF PRIESTLY APOSTASY   1
   Context 3 — The Fourteen Stations 6 — Thomas Merton
   and Padre Pio 24

2 ORDAINED A PRIEST IN DACHAU.   27
   Karl's Life 28 — All for God, Body and Soul 29 — Proud
   to be German 30 — Offering Up His Sufferings 32 —
   A Priest Forever 35

3 HANDLING THE RIGHT BODY.   41
   Abstinent for God's Sake 42 — Spiritual Fatherhood 42 —
   Habeas Corpus 43 — Aiming for God's Body 44 —
   A Loving Exchange 45 — To Give the Sacred 46

4 IN PERSONA CHRISTI   49
   The Person of Christ and Our Person 50 — Ancient Masks
   Offer an Etymology for 'Person' 56 — Martyrdom as the
   Ultimate Identification with Christ 59 — Mental Prayer as
   Union with Christ 64 — Relating to Invisible Persons 67 —
   The Blessed Virgin Mary Configures Priests to Her Son
   Jesus 72

5 UNFOLDING THE HOLY SHROUD   83
   Considering the Holy Shroud 85 — Why Holy Church
   takes her time 86 — God's Love Letter 87 — Truth knows
   no expiration date 88 — The Sense of Faith equips us to
   discern 90 — Filial concern 92

6 PRIESTLY UNITY AND CONCELEBRATION   97
   The holy angels concelebrate 97 — Three Historical
   Meanings of Concelebration 98 — Around the bishop 102 —
   Theological Principles 103 — Six Risks Incurred by
   Systematic Sacramental Concelebration 108 — Signs of

Priestly Unity 111 — The Implicit Shift from Sacramental
to Ceremonial Concelebration 116 — Conclusion 121

7 BUILDING THE BRIDE 123
   Old and New Eve 123 — What the Early Fathers
   Wrote 124 — Was the New Eve in the Upper Room? 125 —
   This is Bone of My Bones 126 — God Built the Rib into a
   Woman 128 — The Eucharistic Building of the Bride 130 —
   A Door for the Bride 131 — Naming the Bride 133

8 CONSECRATED TO GOD, BODY AND SOUL 137
   Discernment 138 — Historical Perspective 144 — The
   Time to Found Has Come 148 — On the priesthood in
   general 155 — On religious life in England (*among many
   other good books*) 155

PREFACE

"IN THE YEAR OF THE LORD 2020, RUMOUR HAD it that priests were weary. Many of them, perhaps, lived on autopilot. Few of the worldly ones still believed in taking their 'career' into their own hands. For how could you rise in society, they thought, when you stood for a Saviour that folks told you never rose from the dead, nor even existed? As to devout priests, they saw no sign of a new Pentecost, far from it. In between, the bulk of us carried on, keeping busy with the new Health & Safety parish regulations, contributing to the latest diocesan pastoral plan and observing the safeguarding rules updated by the Government. We had no objection to looking up the Ten Commandments and even the holy Gospels, when we had a chance.

"In truth, when opening them we could not help being moved on hearing our Lord Jesus Christ commending us to his heavenly Father: *I have manifested thy name to the men whom thou hast given me out of the world. Thine they were, and to me thou gavest them; and they have kept thy word* (Jn 17:6). Not at random, we then felt, had we answered his call. Not by mistake, we knew, did we act in his name. And not in vain, we hoped, did we repeat his words, at Mass, in Confession and all his sacraments.

"The invitation uttered by the bishop at our ordination ceremony, sometimes many years earlier, sounded far-fetched and yet hit home:

> My dear sons, chosen as you are . . . to be consecrated as our helpers, keep yourselves blameless in a life of chastity and sanctity. Be well aware of the sacredness of your duties. Be holy as you deal with holy things. When you celebrate the mystery of the Lord's death, see to it that by mortifying your bodies you rid yourselves of all vice and concupiscence. Let the doctrine

you expound be spiritual medicine for the people of
God. Let the fragrance of your lives be the delight of
Christ's Church, that by your preaching and example
you help to build up the edifice which is the family of
God. May it never come about that we, for promoting
you to so great an office, or you, for taking it on yourselves, should deserve the Lord's condemnation; but
rather may we merit a reward from Him. So let it be
by His grace.[1]

"We knew too well that we failed to correspond to so great a
grace. If we ever forgot our weakness, the media would remind us
of our inadequacy. Our dwindling congregation also would betray
our irrelevance, until a global virus emptied our pews. As to the
Church, well . . . little did we feel her protection and guidance. We
agreed with this statement by the Vicar of Christ:

> The primary and fundamental mission of the Church is
> to be a 'field hospital,' a place of healing, mercy and for-
> giveness, and to be the source of hope for all suffering,
> the desperate, the poor, the sinners, and the discarded.[2]

"Yes, we agreed. Only, rather than being the officers, the staff,
the experts in this 'field hospital,' we priests found that we were
the patients, lying on stretchers, in pain, in doubt and sometimes
in anger."

DESPITE BEING WRITTEN IN THE FIRST MONTHS OF THIS
same year of the Lord 2020, the Preface to this book has so far
used the past tense, as if telling a story, a fictional chronicle. Why
is this? Because we hope that many priests—our brethren—will
not recognise themselves in our portrayal. We trust that not a

1 See traditional Roman Pontifical.
2 General Audience by His Holiness, Pope Francis, August 9, 2017.

few are deeply fulfilled in their relationship with the Lord, with the Church and with souls; and that in return the Sovereign High Priest is well pleased with them. But if at times they go through some dark night, are engulfed by the waves of doubt and tempted with infidelity, we pray that these few reflections might be of assistance. Furthermore, we hear of other brother priests who either fell gravely, or who wonder how they haven't yet capitulated. It is our humble conviction that the sample of traditional doctrines and advice gathered in this little book can revive and deepen their identity as other Christs.

To our lay brothers and sisters we also dedicate this book, to help them better understand, value and support their dear priests, the wounded and the shining ones alike. In particular, we hope that seminarians and young men still discerning their calling might draw inspiration from this short presentation.

We beg for the leniency of the informed reader towards what is not a systematic treatise. Concision led us to reserve for a separate publication the essential topic of the Blessed Virgin Mary and the Priest—although Our Immaculate Lady is referred to in various chapters. Similarly, a thorough assessment of the importance of the Sacred Liturgy in the life and ministry of priests will have to be addressed separately, God willing.

Chapter One is *The Fourteen Stations of Priestly Apostasy*. The slow demise of a fictional priest, following a recent film, is the occasion for detailing various precautions and safeguards which we priests would do well to apply. In Chapter Two, *Ordained a Priest in Dachau*, the beautiful figure of Blessed Karl Leisner proves that Christ can make priests thrive in the worst possible surroundings. In a way, this is the dynamic antidote to the fateful failure assessed in Chapter One. Chapter Three is about *Handling the Right Body*. It explores the deep sacramental motive for priestly celibacy and for the manly fulfilment of the priest in his identification to Christ and his service to the Church. *In Persona Christi* is our longest chapter (Chapter Four). It provides various angles for 'unpacking' the well-known expression that priests act 'in the Person of Christ.' Chapter Five, *Unfolding the Holy Shroud*, refers to the relic of Our Lord's Shroud to illustrate the priestly mission to teach revealed truth with fidelity and persuasiveness. In Chapter Six, we examine *Priestly Unity and Concelebration*. Our non-polemical approach exhorts us priests to discover always more precisely what we really mean to do at Holy Mass. *Building the Bride* is our Chapter Seven. With recourse to exegesis, it shows the correspondence between the shaping of Eve and of the Church. Christ the Bridegroom empowers his priests to fulfil his spousal design. Our eighth and last chapter: *Consecrated to God, Body and Soul*, sets the priesthood within the broader calling to consecrated life, including the religious one. It stimulates reflection and invites young readers in particular to enter the lists with confidence.

We thank you for your interest, reader friend, and we commit this slender opus to our glorious models St John Vianney, St Padre Pio, St John Fisher, St John Henry Newman and all our heavenly intercessors, that it might please Our Lord and Our Lady, and might foster, however modestly, priestly sanctification.

Fr Armand de Malleray, FSSP
Warrington, Cheshire, Easter 2020

1

The Fourteen Stations of Priestly Apostasy

IN THIS CHAPTER WE WILL LOOK AT THE DAN-gers threatening our priesthood. What is in jeopardy, more precisely, is not our priesthood as a spiritual configuration to Christ, but our correct use of it. For we know that our priesthood as a sacramental character will never be lost. It remains in our soul forever. Our priestly character will show on our souls even after death, wherever our liberty takes us—away from God in hell if misused, or to God in heaven if implemented. Thus, the priestly character does remain, but its proper use on earth can be hindered, as we all experience. Let us try to understand the perils in which priests find themselves, looking at recent history. Disheartening as it may seem at first, pointing at the wounds, weaknesses, and dysfunctions of the priesthood must be seen proactively as a diagnosis leading to a happy prognosis; from discovery to full recovery. Encouragingly, in another chapter we will reflect on the means to remedy these difficulties, protecting our priesthood to make it bear abundant fruit through God's grace.

For the purpose of illustration, we will use the film *Silence* by Martin Scorsese,[1] released in 2017 based on the 1966 novel of historical fiction by Shūsaku Endō. Set in seventeenth century Japan, it depicts a young European Jesuit priest's attempt to rescue his former mentor gone missing in suspicious circumstances. Tragically, young Fr Rodrigues fails to bring back the senior priest. What is worse, he follows him in apostasy from the Catholic and even the

---

1 Watching the film is not needed to understand this chapter. In fact, we do not recommend it unless one is endowed with a strong and articulate Catholic faith. Well-formed priests might find the film thought-provoking.

Christian faith! Let us explain why this recent film is relevant to our topic. Soon after its release, a reliable Catholic weekly published an article praising that film for the important questions it raised. The same article, though, failed to expose and to deplore the final apostasy of the main character. The journalist further commented that *Silence* is not set in contemporary America but in seventeenth century Japan, so that the choices facing Fr Rodrigues do not apply to our current situation. We beg to disagree with that opinion.

The novel *Silence* by Endō was written in 1966, in a period when priests left the clerical state and ministry by the thousands.[2] There is more than an analogy between the spiritual and ministerial itinerary of the main character, the Portuguese Jesuit priest in Japan in the film, and the situation in the Church at the time when Endō, himself a Catholic from Japan, was writing his novel. The success of his book indicates that contemporary audiences found in it an echo of their own struggles. Therefore, this historical novel is certainly relevant to modern Catholic clergy and laity. Through the prism of a different historical context, it displays the identity crisis of many modern clerics. Indeed, Fr Rodrigues' arrival on the foggy shores of Japan describes what many a young priest may have felt when beginning his priestly ministry in a modern parish, fresh from ordination. His search for his lost mentor subliminally evokes the candid expectation of younger generations of clerics to have the traditions of the Church passed on to them by their elders. His apostasy, after the example of his former tutor, reveals the heavy responsibility more experienced priests have toward younger ones. When Fr Rodrigues insists on the universal appeal of Catholicism based on the permanence of human nature transcending races and cultures, the Japanese inquisitor objects several times that 'Japan is a swamp where Christianity cannot grow.' Swapping the noun 'modernity' with the name 'Japan,' one hears '*modernity* is a swamp where Christianity cannot grow.' This sounds like the mantra of our

---

2   Not to mention the broader haemorrhage of the mystical Body of Christ in the West, as hundreds of thousands of male and female religious renounced their religious commitments while the lapsation of the laity accelerated.

modern times, under whose spell many clergy have fallen since the Second World War. Admittedly, the modern world often feels like 'a swamp where orthodox Catholicism cannot grow.' But, were the Jewish nation and the Roman Empire more welcoming after the first Pentecost, or for that matter, was Japan itself when St Francis Xavier disembarked and started to evangelise it single-handedly, welcoming dozens of thousands of converts into the Church? In reality, the Japanese inquisitor lies, being the devilish figure he is meant to portray in the film. Fr Rodrigues first unmasked him by reminding him that Christianity was growing superbly in Japan until the government started persecuting it, arresting and torturing clergy and laity. In our transposition where seventeenth century Buddhist Japan stands for post-WWII modernity, the swamp where Christianity cannot grow is not 'modernity,' but 'modernism.' Modernity is the modern world as an era in human history: as such, it is fit for successful evangelisation with time-tested tools. *Modernism* on the contrary is the specific heresy indentified by the Vicar of Christ St Pius X on 8th September 1907 in his encyclical *Pascendi*. Catholicism indeed cannot grow upon such soil because it is fatally poisonous, being 'the synthesis of all heresies.' The novel and the film *Silence* are a chilling illustration of what happens to a priestly soul immersed in modernism.

CONTEXT

Recent history. Looking back, we find that things started to go wrong as early as the 1950s, accelerating in the 1960s and sadly escalating in our own era, the early 2020s. Shūsaku Endō wrote his novel *Silence* just after Vatican II. The latest council lasted from 1962 to 1965 and the novel was released in 1966. In that period the identity crisis affecting priests manifested itself in many ways. Offering a detailed explanation of this complex situation is beyond our scope, but the following example captures the spirit of the times. After the Second World War, in France dozens of 'worker priests' chose to exercise a professional activity with the 'proletariat' in factories: not to preach the Good News explicitly, but to reach out to workers by becoming workers in their turn.

This experience was ended by Pope Pius XII in 1953 because it had proved unsuccessful at converting the mass of workers, while at the same time it undermined the consecrated identity of priests. Out of ninety worker priests, nearly thirty had got married or had officially become members of the Communist Party. In 1959 Pope John XXIII ruled against the experiment, but his personal acquaintance with the worker priests experiment as former Nuncio in France (1944–1953) is said to have influenced his concern for 'adapting the Church to the modern world' when convoking the Second Vatican Council. In 1965, Pope Paul VI allowed worker priests again. Admittedly, their numbers were very small in proportion with the overall Catholic clergy. But their aspirations were shared by many priests worldwide. In *Silence*, the demise by stages of the mentor Jesuit and of his disciple, embracing Buddhism and dropping celibacy, echoes this trend.

At the same time in Latin America, the so-called Theology of Liberation led many priests to consider that their mission was essentially to be political awakeners — meaning, Marxist inculcators. This again influenced the clergy even very far from Latin America, as the following example shows. The author grew up in Western France, in a small village on the north bank of the Loire River. This area used to be strongly Catholic, as demonstrated by the fact that several parish priests there had died as martyrs during the anti-Catholic French Revolution. In the early 1980s though, worship and doctrine changed rapidly when the old parish priest, 'Monsieur le Curé,' was forced to retire. The author's grandmother was very involved in the parish where she used to play the harmonium (a tiny mechanical organ). One Sunday morning, she found the church sanctuary adorned with long black cow chains. 'Surely,' she reflected 'some deep Christian symbol must be offered here. These chains probably represent the chains of sin.' She had guessed correctly, but only up to a point. The homily soon enlightened her, as the newly appointed priest explained that those were 'the chains of capitalism, the capital sin against humanity.' The self-promulgated 'rubrics' of the clerical 'opening to the world' were strictly abided by as the priests wore lay clothes only, insisted on being addressed by their first name without any clerical title, displayed marked casualness in their offering of Holy Mass, demanding lay activity in the sanctuary, while waging war against dogmas that 'hindered the (Holy?) Spirit.' All this sounds rather ordinary to us in 2020, but coming after centuries of priestly reverence, it was a spectacular novelty in the 1980s. Priests came to understand themselves as sociologists, as community animators, as political activists, but no longer as sacrificers, that is, as men of the sacred, acting *in Persona Christi*.

What the numbers tell us. Let us now look at how broad figures confirm this loss of priestly identity. The local territorial parish led by a priest on behalf of the diocesan bishop had long been the official unit defining the sacramental and ecclesial life of individual Catholics. But in 2014, 22% of the Catholic parishes worldwide did not have a resident priest as pastor anymore.[3] Since no parish was ever established without a priest pastor to lead it, the figure means that about 50,000 parishes worldwide had lost their resident pastor. What led to that? Between 1970 and 2012 the number of priests declined from 419,000 roughly to 414,000. The drop in absolute numbers may not seem spectacular, but we must note three things. The first remark is that this figure is global, thus encompassing huge discrepancies between more stable areas and others marked by very severe plummeting, particularly in the Western world where the number of clergy was so high and well established. Second, the

---

3 Precisely 49,153 parishes out of 221,740 were without a resident priest pastor in 2014. It was an improvement from 1995, when over a quarter of worldwide parishes, namely 27.58%, were priestless. But in the West at least, those figures concealed a more alarming reality: the amalgamating of parishes, which simply grouped as one new canonical entity several priestless parishes up to then distinct. In other words, the decrease from 27% to 22% priestless parishes worldwide between 1995 and 2014 is likely to reflect not an increase of resident pastors, but a suppression of priestless parishes. Meanwhile, the percentage of Catholics in the world population remained remarkably stable at 17.5% between 1970 and 2014. With the halving of priests, this figure further indicates that non Catholics and pagans are only half as likely to meet a Catholic priest to bring them to the only ark of salvation, the Holy Catholic Church founded by Christ. For figures see https://web.archive.org/web/20160120072339/http:/cara.georgetown.edu/caraservices/requestedchurchstats.html, accessed 8th July 2019.

figure spans a large amount of time: 42 years, during which this priestly generation grew older, i.e. less active, because physically less strong. But the third and main observation is that this drop in the number of priests, about 6,000 worldwide, must be contrasted with the increase in Catholic population which nearly doubled over the same period from 653,000,000 worldwide in 1970 to twice that amount in 2012, namely 1,229,000,000. The alarming consequence is that the ratio — the number of Catholics per priest globally — was in 1980, one priest for 1,895 Catholics; while in 2012 it was one priest for 3,126 Catholics. This is almost twice the original amount. In proportion then, there are approximately half as many priests now as there were in 1970. Although one should not overestimate the accuracy of global statistics, and while making allowance for different interpretations of the figures, the overall trend evidenced seems reliable.

With this *caveat*, let us apply our findings to a few practical situations presented in general terms for Western Catholics in particular. If in the 1970s it used to take you fifteen minutes to drive to your nearest church, it should now take you half an hour. Or, if you relied on a confessor available to restore God's grace to your soul, you are now half as likely to find one to reconcile you with God. Further, if Holy Mass used to be offered every Sunday at your church, it would now be offered every other Sunday. Lastly, if you expected to die fortified by the Last Rites of the Church, the risk is now fifty percent higher of your dying without a priest to prepare your soul for judgement, and without a funeral Mass offered for your soul's eternal rest, assuming you die in a state of grace. Such figures confirm that Endō's novel is not merely about 'the personal itinerary of one missionary in 17th-century Japan' but tragically applies to the modern Church and to not a few clerics.

THE FOURTEEN STATIONS

With this in mind, we can now look at the film itself and go through the stages of what we call the fourteen stations of priestly apostasy. These are a modern counterpart of the Fourteen Stations of the Way of the Cross, walked in Jerusalem by the Sovereign High

Priest Jesus Christ to Calvary in the year 33. The difference is that the innocent Lord bore no responsibility for the sins he expiated on our behalf; whereas our fourteen stations depict the culpable demise of priests into sins they freely commit.

Generally speaking, the underground Catholics in the novel and in the film, that is, the Japanese lay people, display more faith than the Portuguese Jesuit priest himself. He seems always to be lagging behind them as regards the expression of his faith. Problematically, he does not feel embarrassed by his undue restraint. We do not hear him wish he had their courage or devotion. On the contrary, he seems to find that the faith of his simple flock is somehow superstitious and needs enlightenment. Regrettably, such mindset was shared by many clerics in the 1970s, and possibly still is in the West.

Let us now review some episodes and circumstances in the film. We should like to stress that we are not in the least claiming that the novelist, or the film director, or their character Fr Rodrigues himself meant to use these incidents to describe an 'apostasy.' We are only interpreting the scenario as a parable to help us in our observations, for the sake of the priestly identity.

Station I: Skip grace before meals. In the film, the first omen is that the priest skips grace before meals. Having just arrived in Japan and disembarked, he is welcomed into the underground Church where poor hidden Catholics treat him to a very frugal meal—all that these peasant people have to share. After he has started eating, he notices that they are waiting, and that they soon recite some prayers before the meal. This is a very small thing, as skipping grace before meal is obviously not apostasy. But it reveals something in that priest. Already, in Fr Rodrigues, we note a lack of awareness about the need to sanctify all that he does, performing it in the name of God. From the start, the young missionary fails to lead his flock by example, sanctifying the most routine and ordinary events of the day.

Station II: Part with rosary beads. Fr Rodrigues parts with his rosary beads. In the film, again, this occurs with a good intention. Due to his condition as a clandestine visitor to Japan, his lean bag is bereft of any artefacts of Christian art or of devotional items to share. Seeing the underground Catholics so devoid of any such objects of piety and anxious to obtain some, Fr Rodrigues breaks up his rosary, generously handing one separate bead to each Christian. But, again, if we transpose this to the modern era, many priests looked down on praying the Holy Rosary, thinking it a superstitious practice; or at best a custom 'for uneducated people' whereas 'they [the priests] commune directly with God and don't need such rigid and repetitive prayers.' Happy would such priests be if their faith in Our Lady's role of leading them to her Son had not been damaged.

Station III: Ignore vestments. Fr Rodrigues offers Holy Mass. Film-director Scorsese designed a rather beautiful picture or sequence, when the missionary says Mass towards East in a hidden room, very much like here in England under Protestant persecution during Penal Times, or in Communist and Muslim countries until now. Again, for the purposes of our account, we observe that he is not wearing vestments to say Mass. There are good reasons in the film for this, as he has no belongings with him. He uses the bare minimum, that is a missal and a very small chalice, and some hosts and wine. But again, this echoes a tendency which we have witnessed or read about, when the previous generation of priests started taking liberties with the rubrics, which they resented as something restricting their creativity. They consequently did away with, for instance, the wearing of vestments or at least some of them; and ceased pronouncing only the words printed in black in the altar missal.

Station IV: Don't push for baptism. Fr Rodrigues performs his first direct pastoral ministry after Holy Mass, namely, the baptism of a child. There is something ambiguous in his perception of the event. The impression conveyed is that of a discrepancy between pastor and flock. The parents of the newly baptized child express their joy that their child is now saved as a child of God. By contrast, the priest does not really understand their joy, and he distances himself from the parents' statement that now the child is under God's protection, and saved as a child of God. The priest seems to imply that things are not so simple. Again, we are not entering here into a theological debate on the necessity of sacramental baptism, or on the difficulties of actually developing our Christian life. But we refer to Fr Rodrigues' reaction in the film as one more step in the stations of apostasy. Many a priest may be tempted to see the rites of the Church as something a bit too simple, too obvious, too easy. Some priests may forget and later question the doctrine of *ex opere operato* which teaches that the sacraments, when performed according to the rubrics and intention of the Church, do actually achieve what they signify, conferring grace. They may lose sight of the dogma according to which, being made an adopted child of God through holy Baptism — the *ianua sacramentorum*, gate of all the sacraments — is a condition for salvation, as God has not revealed to us any other means. In principle, the baptism of desire and even the implicit desire of baptism can save the soul of a pagan in good faith. But sacramental baptism is the only formal means revealed to us by Christ. Therefore a missionary must do everything to provide this means and it is a duty binding clergy even in non-mission territories.

Station V: Lie in bed. The priest fails to get up on time. Admittedly, this is unfair to the characters and the scenario, since Fr Rodrigues and his confrere are forced to hide in a shed during interminable days so as to avoid detection and arrest. Only by night do they venture outdoors, and with extreme caution. But their situation can be transposed as an illustration of the contempt shown by many modern clerics for traditional asceticism. Some think that modern times demand of them flexibility and inventiveness, at the expense of discipline and of a rule of life. Prudent guidelines such as fixed times for getting out of bed in the morning and for switching off the light at night were discarded as hindrances to pastoral zeal. The wisdom of ages dictating early rising and no late nights (outside of occasional sick calls) was scorned. In the film *Silence*, it is another step toward apostasy. The issue at stake for priests in general is not laziness as such, although that might be part of the problem, but rather imprudence. It betrays a lack of trust in the experience of the ages in setting for ourselves a daily schedule. At the very bottom, we reluctantly identify pride, insofar as priests dispensing with a daily routine think themselves cleverer and stronger than our fallen human nature ordinarily shows itself to be.

Station VI: Leave priestly company. Fr Rodrigues parts with
priestly company. There were two of them, two young Jesuits,
arriving in Japan together. The confrere of Fr Rodrigues decides
to visit another village. This is a valid reason as far as the story
goes, since it enables them to reach out to more souls. But as a
result, each of them finds himself alone. Even though there may
be a few members of the faithful where each one hides, there is no
fellow-cleric anymore to provide support in watchful and caring
fraternity. This fraternal support has been lost in recent decades,
sadly. Living among fellow priests was once considered a need, a
precaution and a boon. Admittedly, the priesthood is something
particularized, since our soul received the priestly character individually, and it is as individuals that we will give an account to
God for the use we will have made of priestly graces. But we are
supported by being part of a *presbyterium,* striving together for
holiness daily, not only once a year at a Mass with the bishop. We
need fraternal care and encouragement on a daily basis. This would
mean certainly, wherever possible, leading a communal life, not
only for religious clergy, or Oratorians, but also for secular clergy
in parishes.[4] We confess that living alone is more comfortable. One
can watch whatever one pleases on television and for as long as
one wants. One can drink and eat what one prefers in the quantity
one fancies. One can let in visitors of either sex at the time one
prefers. This offers many options indeed, but at the expense of
prudence and often of the integrity of the priestly life. We are not
suggesting that every priest who lives alone falls into mortal sin,
or that priests living in common are *ipso facto* confirmed in grace.
We are merely stating prudential rules found helpful by previous
generations. The fact that the majority of us priests nowadays live

4   'The annals of the Church show that at times when priests generally
lived in a form of common life, this association produced many good results.
Why might not one re-establish in our own day something of the kind, with
due attention to differences of country and priestly duties? Might not one
justifiably hope, and the Church would rejoice at it, that such an institution
would yield the same good results as formerly?' Cf. Encyclical *Haerent Animo,*
by Pope St Pius X, 4th August 1908.

alone in big presbyteries or in anonymous blocks of flats does not strengthen our priestly identity. A consequence of it is the loneliness of many priests who feel unsupported, not understood or cared about. Most communication priests receive from fellow clergy is purely administrative. They don't feel valued chiefly for the sake of the divine imprint which marked their immortal souls at ordination. They may gradually lose sight of the central truth defining them as 'other Christs,' standing *in persona Christi* at the altar where they offer the Divine Victim; and sitting at the tribunal of mercy in the confessional reconciling penitents with God.

Station VII: Stop offering Mass. Fr Rodrigues stops offering the Holy Mass. Once again, the scenario fully justifies this change. After having escaped the Japanese police for weeks, the unfortunate priest is betrayed by an apostate Catholic. The guards who arrest him search the bag he is carrying. They extract from it a Mass kit with a small chalice and the few other items strictly required to offer Holy Mass. All these are confiscated by the authorities. It is obviously not Fr Rodrigues' choice not to offer Holy Mass anymore in the film. But as an illustration of the crisis affecting modern clergy, this seventh Station is a most alarming symptom. Admittedly, a priest is not bound in principle to offer the Holy Sacrifice of the Mass daily. But since offering Mass is essential to priestly calling, a serious obligation applies. The weekly day off does not dispense from it, neither do holidays. Thus, it's problematic when a priest fails to offer Holy Mass without a proportionately grave reason. Offering the Holy Sacrifice of the Mass is the most important thing happening in the world every day: not only for a priest, not only for Catholics, but for whoever fits the definition of 'human being,' that is, fallen children of Adam and Eve. The reason for this is that the Holy Sacrifice of the Mass is the application of Christ's merits to our souls. Christ acquired all merits to save us when he died on the Cross. But such costly remedies still need to be applied to individual souls throughout space and time. By divine institution, the chief mode for this vital application is the

offering of Holy Mass as frequently as the needs of souls require.[5]
A priest who neglects this frustrates the salvation of souls, thus
betraying a flawed understanding of his priestly identity.

Station VIII: Drop the habit. The loss of clerical attire. In
Silence again, the scenario accounts for this. The guards and the
officials give Fr Rodrigues a very elegant silk robe to put on while
in prison. It is an indigenous kind of clothing, and clean, unlike the
ragged cassock he wore up to then. But the visual distinctiveness
of his clerical identity is then taken away from him. He now only
looks like a Japanese among other Japanese. Sadly we know too
well that this is exactly what happened in the 1970s and from then
on. First in the West, and later on nearly everywhere, priests were
persuaded that, to be closer to the people, they needed to get rid
of whatever could be seen as a separation, as a screen, anything
emphasizing their priesthood as a status, lest it deter people from
opening up to them. If this concern had any foundation in reality,
one really wonders how, to take a couple of emblematic examples,
the Curé of Ars and St John Bosco attracted thousands. Most people in their times were certainly not devout, not even Christian. In
nineteenth century industrial Turin or in post-French Revolution
Bellay and Ars, the faith was not deeply rooted, but questioned,
and sometimes openly opposed. And yet, St John Marie Vianney
and St John Bosco were able to attract thousands and thousands of
souls, some of them not believers, some lapsed, lost and in search
for the truth. These priests were not wearing lay dress but a black
cassock. Significantly, the *Directory on the Ministry and Life of
Priests*[6] states that the cassock is the standard clerical attire, from

5   *Quoties hujus hostiae commemoratio celebratur, opus nostrae redemptionis exercetur.* As often as the commemoration of this victim is celebrated,
the work of our redemption is performed. Secret prayer of the 9th Sunday
after Pentecost, Extraordinary Form Roman Missal; quoted in the Ordinary
Form Roman Missal's GIRM #2.

6   Cf. *Directory on the Ministry and Life of Priests*, Congregation for the
Clergy, Copyright Libreria Editrice Vaticana, 31st January 1994, #66, *Obligation
of Ecclesiastical Attire*:

'In a secularised and materialistic society, where the external signs of sacred
and supernatural realities tend to disappear, it is particularly important that

which exceptions can be envisaged. The cassock is sacral, whereas the clerical suit is utilitarian. Furthermore, the cassock shows even under an overcoat, whereas it only takes a scarf to conceal a Roman collar. It is not our purpose to discuss further the shapes and patterns of clerical attire, provided they manifest the priestly identity of the wearer constantly and unambiguously. Here in England, our very first martyr was Saint Alban, who died probably in 209 near London to save a priest visitor, putting on his guest's attire. Whatever that priestly garb looked like, it was distinctive enough for the Roman pursuers to identify Alban as the hunted man of God, mistaking him with the cleric who thus escaped to minister further to souls. Outside times of open persecution, the clerical attire is a protection for us priests, an opportunity for the people and a message to the world.

Station IX: Haunt the beach. An onlooker at the beach. Sheltered by a screen from the mild breeze, Fr Rodrigues rests on a folding chair, facing the sea. His smooth Japanese gown loosely tightened, his hands rest on the warm sand, while his dilated nostrils inhale rushes of salty air sent by the nearby waves. What could have been an idyllic siesta soon ends though, when the shrieks

---

the community be able to recognise the priest, man of God and dispenser of his mysteries, by his attire as well, which is an unequivocal sign of his dedication and his identity as a public minister. The priest should be identifiable primarily through his conduct, but also by his manner of dressing, which makes visible to all the faithful, indeed and to all men, his identity and his belonging to God and the Church.

'For this reason, the clergy should wear "suitable ecclesiastical dress, in accordance with the norms established by the Episcopal Conference and the legitimate local custom." This means that the attire, when it is not the cassock, must be different from the manner in which the laity dress, and conform to the dignity and sacredness of his ministry. The style and colour should be established by the Episcopal Conference, always in agreement with the dispositions of the universal law.

'Because of their incoherence with the spirit of this discipline, contrary practices cannot be considered legitimate customs; and should be removed by the competent authority.

'Outside of entirely exceptional cases, a cleric's failure to use this proper ecclesiastical attire could manifest a weak sense of his identity as one consecrated to God.'

of fellow Christians — not of seagulls — pierce his eardrums. Fr Rodrigues is forced to witness the martyrdom of his flock and fellow Jesuit priest being drowned by executioners in the water. Thankfully, we modern priests ordinarily don't come across executions when resting by the sea. But this tragic episode in the film *Silence* can be compared with our lives for the sake of examining how we spend our leisure. What are our recreations? Where do we go when we are not at the altar, or in the confessional, or shopping for groceries? How do we spend our day off? Where do we go for holiday, and what exactly do we do there? In the past, some priests have received many graces while at a beach. Wasn't it by the shore of the Sea of Galilee that Our Blessed Lord organised a picnic after his resurrection, with his own hands preparing fish for his apostles? However, at holiday resorts, beaches tend to be populated with sirens rather than apostles. A priest should think thrice before sitting in their company, lest his consecrated soul drown. Exceptions may occur, such as by a swimming pool in the exclusive family circle, or an early swim on a deserted beach or with fellow-clerics. Priests simply need to assess before the Lord if a given leisure activity recreates or desecrates their body and soul. Wherever we go, whether to a cinema, or to a restaurant, or to a musical or on a cruise, we must always honour Christ. We are always ambassadors of Christ, even on holiday, so that our glorious priesthood, which is a gift for the world, must be neither hidden nor sullied.

Station X: Bow to jargon. Fr Rodrigues is overwhelmed by academic jargon. The exhausted priest finally meets with his former mentor, who by then is a persuasive apostate. This encounter is engineered by the Japanese officials to shake the intellectual certainties of their Christian prisoner. The former-Jesuit-turned-Buddhist affirms to Fr Rodrigues that his native flock was mistaken from the start because a flawed translation was taught them. When the first Jesuit missionaries preached about 'God the Son,' the Japanese understood 'God the Sun,' which is one of their main pagan deities. Never understanding Christ, they never actually embraced Catholicism. Was it all in vain, then? 'No,' says the tempter, instilling the poison of relativism and syncretism into the mind of his former disciple. Contrasting his deep knowledge of the Japanese culture with the superficial grasp Fr Rodrigues has of it, he states that the theological misunderstanding never really mattered, because the hearts of the natives were genuinely geared towards worship anyway. Later on, he explains, his scientific discoveries led him to a critical reviewing of the Catholic faith as merely one among the various paths to 'superior knowledge.'

Faithful Catholics know that faith and reason share truth as their common object, hence the Church's spearheading of support to the sciences, from the scriptoria in early monasteries to the creation of the first universities. However, unfortunately, since the nineteenth century, sacred sciences such as exegesis, theology, biblical archaeology and liturgy have often been twisted to undermine the faith. From the noble pursuit and service of truth, they were degraded into ideological tools. Under the guise of scientific expertise, many clergy have, in fact, poisoned the sincere faith of several generations. They were not truly speaking in the name of Christ and the Church. They displayed academic titles and gained influence through impressive publications, silencing the humble, including the 'lower clergy.' Too many of these shut their mouths and simply believed that they were being superstitious and naïve, since those learned clerics with the doctorates and the jargon surely knew better.

This was certainly an effect of the Modernist crisis as identified by Pope St Pius X in his 1907 encyclical *Pascendi*, and powerfully restrained from 1910 onwards through his Anti-modernist Oath,[7]

---

7   'I . . . firmly embrace and accept each and every definition that has been set forth and declared by the unerring teaching authority of the Church, especially those principal truths which are directly opposed to the errors of this day. And first of all, I profess that God, the origin and end of all things, can be known with certainty by the natural light of reason from the created world (see Rom. 1:19), that is, from the visible works of creation, as a cause from its effects, and that, therefore, his existence can also be demonstrated: Secondly, I accept and acknowledge the external proofs of revelation, that is, divine acts and especially miracles and prophecies as the surest signs of the divine origin of the Christian religion and I hold that these same proofs are well adapted to the understanding of all eras and all men, even of this

time. Thirdly, I believe with equally firm faith that the Church, the guardian and teacher of the revealed word, was personally instituted by the real and historical Christ when he lived among us, and that the Church was built upon Peter, the prince of the apostolic hierarchy, and his successors for the duration of time. Fourthly, I sincerely hold that the doctrine of faith was handed down to us from the apostles through the orthodox Fathers in exactly the same meaning and always in the same purport. Therefore, I entirely reject the heretical misrepresentation that dogmas evolve and change from one meaning to another different from the one which the Church held previously. I also condemn every error according to which, in place of the divine deposit which has been given to the spouse of Christ to be carefully guarded by her, there is put a philosophical figment or product of a human conscience that has gradually been developed by human effort and will continue to develop indefinitely. Fifthly, I hold with certainty and sincerely confess that faith is not a blind sentiment of religion welling up from the depths of the subconscious under the impulse of the heart and the motion of a will trained to morality; but faith is a genuine assent of the intellect to truth received by hearing from an external source. By this assent, because of the authority of the supremely truthful God, we believe to be true that which has been revealed and attested to by a personal God, our creator and lord.

'Furthermore, with due reverence, I submit and adhere with my whole heart to the condemnations, declarations, and all the prescripts contained in the encyclical *Pascendi* and in the decree *Lamentabili,* especially those concerning what is known as the history of dogmas. I also reject the error of those who say that the faith held by the Church can contradict history, and that Catholic dogmas, in the sense in which they are now understood, are irreconcilable with a more realistic view of the origins of the Christian religion. I also condemn and reject the opinion of those who say that a well-educated Christian assumes a dual personality—that of a believer and at the same time of a historian, as if it were permissible for a historian to hold things that contradict the faith of the believer, or to establish premises which, provided there be no direct denial of dogmas, would lead to the conclusion that dogmas are either false or doubtful. Likewise, I reject that method of judging and interpreting Sacred Scripture which, departing from the tradition of the Church, the analogy of faith, and the norms of the Apostolic See, embraces the misrepresentations of the rationalists and with no prudence or restraint adopts textual criticism as the one and supreme norm. Furthermore, I reject the opinion of those who hold that a professor lecturing or writing on a historico-theological subject should first put aside any preconceived opinion about the supernatural origin of Catholic tradition or about the divine promise of help to preserve all revealed truth forever; and that they should then interpret the writings of each of the Fathers solely by scientific principles, excluding all sacred authority, and with the same liberty of judgement that is common in the investigation of all ordinary historical documents.

a detailed repudiation of the modern errors 'to be sworn to by all clergy, pastors, confessors, preachers, religious superiors, and professors in philosophical-theological seminaries.' The anti-modernist oath was abolished in 1967 by Pope Paul VI (a year earlier, Endō had released his novel *Silence*).

Being a combination of many errors, the modernist heresy is difficult to synthesize. The following is offered as a sample of its *errors*. The Gospel writers often narrated non-historical events. Instead, they gave precedence to what they deemed spiritually useful to the early Christians. This leads to distinguishing between the 'Christ of history' and the 'Christ of faith.' For instance, the Resurrection is not an historical event, it is a faith event. Also, Christ was not aware of his divinity from the start. Perhaps later on, the feeling of it grew stronger and at the end, that led him to give up his life. Surely Christ did not mean to establish his Church as a visible and permanent institution. What he envisaged was the Kingdom of heaven here and now. Finally, dogmas are not immutable. They must change not only in formulation, but also in meaning, to suit the concerns and aspirations of new generations of believers and also to reflect the progress of sciences.

'Finally, I declare that I am completely opposed to the error of the modernists who hold that there is nothing divine in sacred tradition; or what is far worse, say that there is, but in a pantheistic sense, with the result that there would remain nothing but this plain simple fact—one to be put on a par with the ordinary facts of history—the fact, namely, that a group of men by their own labour, skill, and talent have continued through subsequent ages a school begun by Christ and his apostles. I firmly hold, then, and shall hold to my dying breath the belief of the Fathers in the charism of truth, which certainly is, was, and always will be in the succession of the episcopacy from the apostles. The purpose of this is, then, not that dogma may be tailored according to what seems better and more suited to the culture of each age; rather, that the absolute and immutable truth preached by the apostles from the beginning may never be believed to be different, may never be understood in any other way.

'I promise that I shall keep all these articles faithfully, entirely, and sincerely, and guard them inviolate, in no way deviating from them in teaching or in any way in word or in writing. Thus I promise, this I swear, so help me God...'

We suggest that this lethal process is well illustrated by Station Ten of our paradigm of apostasy, as inspired by the film *Silence*. Fr Rodrigues had been weakened by the loss of many defences (devotional, liturgical, ascetical, fraternal, vestimentary), but losing his intellectual confidence undermines him more fatally. Why witness the suffering of native converts if the Catholic creed they die for is but one valid option among many? Why confess Christ at the cost of one's comfort, freedom and life if worshipping a sun god pleases the deity just as well? On the contrary, Catholic means *universal*, so that our divinely revealed creed applies to all without any exception, invalidating any contrary belief.

Station XI: Fill your stomach. A feast for the stomach. Fr Rodrigues' gaolers treat him to an elaborate dinner. If applied to the life of modern clergy, there is nothing reprehensible. Eating well has a bearing on body and mind. It is also an important aspect of clerical conviviality. For example, on Maundy Thursday, some priests will go out for lunch to a nice restaurant with fellow clergy, as a way of celebrating the institution of the priesthood. But vigilance still applies to make sure that we use food and drink as the means they should remain, rather than become addicted to them. In penitential seasons, sobriety and fasting lead us deeper into God. The cunning of our adversary the devil is more surely exposed and defeated when our bodily urges are kept under gentle but firm control. Fr Rodrigues is aware of the risk when the appetizing food is laid before him. He challenges his guard, noticing that they expect to weaken his will. As it happens, he welcomes the food as a distraction from his many problems. Coming after the onslaught on his intellectual confidence, the attack by means of his stomach proves a clever tactical move on the part of his enemies.

Station XII: Trust emotions. Fr Rodrigues bases his faith on sensory experience. The Japanese inquisitor — with the apostate Jesuit — assures Fr Rodrigues that his parishioners will not suffer torture any longer if he merely agrees to trample upon a picture of Christ on the floor. The prisoner priest resists until he believes that he hears the voice of Christ telling him to trample upon the depiction of his Sacred Face. This alleged locution convinces Fr

Rodrigues that God truly wants him to offer the sign required to save his parishioners. On the contrary, for months past, he had sought in vain to hear the voice of Christ to guide his mission. Instead of the divine voice, he had perceived only silence, frustratingly. He wrongly relied on sensorial experience to support his faith and inform his decision. He forgot that our Catholic faith is essentially based on the series of the articles in the Creed, that is, of objective data which our intellect can and must understand as true; then learn and memorize; so that our will may adhere to it as to something good, helped in that by the grace of God. Faith, contrary to the claim of the modernist heresy, does not depend on feelings and emotions. God may grant these as encouragements when beneficial to us, but they do not determine the validity of our faith.

Station XIII: Give up on signs. Some intelligent people believe that if truth exists, it cannot be objectively expressed through words and other signs. According to this error, a human individual may commune with truth internally, but attempting to express truth to fellow humans in a shared understanding of objective reality is impossible and futile. If one's heart is well-disposed, subjectively, then no sign really matters. In the film, the sign presented to Fr Rodrigues is the embossed Holy Face of Christ. The gesture expected of him is to trample the sacred item. This gesture has an objective meaning, namely, the repudiating of the divinity of Christ. The unfortunate missionary finally tramples upon the picture of Christ. He is told that this is 'just a formality.' He accepts the lie according to which trampling the sacred artefact leaves unharmed in his soul the loving presence of the divine Original.

He is utterly wrong. His foot has truly kicked God out of his own person. His conversion to Buddhism is also a repudiation of philosophical realism, giving up on signs. He accepts the claim that signs bear no relation to the truth, which can be adhered to internally only. He succumbs to this lie as a consequence (by anticipation) of the modernist heresy which has already seduced him intellectually. Indeed, once one admits a distinction between the 'Christ of faith' present in the heart of this missionary, and the 'Christ of history' represented by the cast depiction of the

Saviour, one can trample upon the Christ of history, because the real Christ is assumed to be the one of personal emotions, the one of subjective beliefs, living only within the privacy of the believer's heart, unscathed by external gestures and words — or so the voice assures when after months of so-called silence, Fr Rodrigues hears: 'Trample upon me'...

What if a Sacred Host had been laid on the floor instead of a mere image of Christ? Would Fr Rodrigues have trampled it? Yes, he would have: based on his philosophical error according to which signs are incapable of expressing invisible realities, the Holy Eucharist as a sign[8] could be defaced without actually harming Christ. Can we apply this to our modern circumstances? The noticeable lack of reverence towards the Holy Eucharist displayed by many priests betrays a loss of sacramental belief. As Catholic ministers in good standing, rather than proclaimed desecrators, they cannot mean to offend God, especially not in the public display of the official liturgy. Their carelessness in handling the consecrated species only makes sense if in their eyes, the Eucharistic signs are disconnected from the divine presence.[9]

Station XIV: Go places. Then all unfolds, or unravels, rather. The new apostate is rewarded with a comfortable house and a sweat-free job consisting in seeking out depictions of Christ and Our Lady and the Saints. Daily, he checks artefacts extracted from the crates of Western merchants and, whenever detecting Christian patterns, he has the item taken away and destroyed. When we look at so many churches built since the 1960s and when we compare them with what used to be understood as a traditional Catholic setting for worship and devotion, we discover an alarming loss. Depictions of Christ, Our Lady, the angels and saints,

---

8   While Eucharistic irreverence does not harm Christ physically, it gravely offends him through spurning his salvific presence.

9   'Many see communion as a purely ceremonial gesture' cf. *Open Letter in Klerusblatt* by Pope Emeritus Benedict XVI, April 10, 2019. The word 'abuse' occurs thirty-four times in the Vatican Instruction *Redemptionis Sacramentum: On certain matters to be observed or to be avoided regarding the Most Holy Eucharist*, released on 25 March 2004.

have disappeared — a real iconoclastic crisis! The rare new ones are often unspiritual, ugly to look at, and sometimes frightening, like Christ's *Resurrection* by Pericle Fazzini, commissioned by Pope Paul VI himself for the new Vatican hall inaugurated in 1977. There are exceptions, thankfully. Here in England, outside Portsmouth Cathedral for example, stands a beautiful statue of St John the Evangelist. Although modern, it is elegant and inspiring. Generally speaking though, true, genuine and eloquent depictions of our faith through sacred art have become very rare.

Apostasy does not only save Fr Rodrigues' (mortal) life: it also secures for him material comfort, a wife and a social position. Discarding his priestly celibacy seals Fr Rodrigues' new status. The sacrifice of marital intimacy and of family life by priests is a most potent factor of configuration to Christ the Sovereign Priest. Christ was celibate and the priesthood is fittingly expressed through celibacy because priests stand in the person of Christ the divine Bridegroom, who is married to the Church. Priests speak and act in his name in deeper conformity to their model when known to entertain no exclusive love for a wife and children. On the contrary, these favours are granted Fr Rodrigues by the Japanese inquisitor as a reward for his contribution to the official culture at the expense of Catholicism.

What neither the novel nor the film mentions is that the Japanese Inquisitor Inoue Masashige, a historical figure, was a powerful promoter of homosexuality.[10] Present in Japan in 1648–1654, the Swedish merchant Olof Eriksson Willman reported in his *Journal* the advances toward him by Inoue.[11] This detail resonates in our

---

10   Since nominalism denies the reality of natures, including the human nature, how could it see homosexuality as un*natural*? The obvious fact that human beings share constant characteristics both physical and psychological, such as an innate sexed identity distinguishing them as men and women, is seen by nominalists as accidental. Nature for them is not a principle of growth granted by a wise Creator, but raw material to feed any fanciful appetites.

11   Willman's *Journal* is consistent with the findings of St Francis Xavier himself: *In my view, the ordinary lay people commit fewer sins and are more obedient to reason than those they call Bonzes and regard as their spiritual fathers. The Bonzes are addicted to unnatural vice, and readily admit it, for*

modern era where clerics are allured with the rewards of popu-
larity and preferment if they become complicit with the prevailing
culture of death. It is not irrelevant that the priest whose guidance
on Jesuit spirituality was sought by film director Scorsese for his
film *Silence* was Fr James Martin SJ, well known for his zealous
attempts to make inversion accepted by the Church.[12]

Having died of old age, the apostate priest is burned in a bucket
according to the rules and customs of the godless spirituality he
had embraced, Buddhism in his case.[13] An invention of Scorsese
was to put a small crucifix in the hands of the corpse surrounded
with flames. Even if this detail had been part of Endō's original
story, it would have been radically insufficient to rescind Rodrigues'
apostasy. A Christian artefact concealed after death within a pagan
rite of cremation does not as if by magic absolve an apostate priest.
A public retraction would have been needed. God warned us, *Every
one therefore that shall confess me before men, I will also confess
him before my Father who is in heaven. But he that shall deny me
before men, I will also deny him before my Father who is in heaven*
(Mt 10:32–33).

Our fourteen stations of priestly apostasy are offered as a warning. They detail the historical circumstances through which Fr
Rodrigues, a fictional priest, went through in the film *Silence* by

---

*it is so notorious and well known to everybody that men and women of every
condition take it for granted and show no abhorrence of it. Still, the laity are
very pleased to hear us denounce this abominable sin* ... St Francis Xavier
S.J., first apostle of Japan, cf. Schurhammer, *Epistolae S. Francisci Xaverii*,
ii, 179–88 — quoted by James Broderick S.J., *Saint Francis Xavier* (London:
Burnes & Oates 1952), 362–63.

12   Fr Martin travelled from New York to St Beuno's Jesuit Centre in
North Wales, United Kingdom, to give the Ignatian Exercises to the two
Hollywood actors playing the unfortunate Jesuits in the film *Silence*. Fr Martin
has over half a million 'friends' on Facebook. In April 2017 he was appointed
consultor to the Vatican's communications office and in 2018 he was invited
as speaker to the (Catholic) World Meeting of Families in Dublin.

13   Buddhism entails no belief in a personal god.

Scorsese. We know well that, sadly, his decline has been replicated on a large scale since the 1960s, all over the world, for so many priests. The fourteen stations can be summarised as follows:

1. failing to sanctify ordinary actions, e.g. skipping grace before meals
2. abandoning traditional devotions such as the Holy Rosary
3. not wearing the prescribed vestments for Holy Mass
4. not asserting the power of the sacraments *ex opere operato*
5. not observing a stable routine, in particular as regards bed time
6. not wanting priestly company, especially for sharing house
7. ceasing to offer Holy Mass daily
8. doing away with clerical attire even on 'working days'
9. concealing one's priesthood at leisure times
10. bowing to academic novelties at the expenses of traditional doctrine
11. denying one's stomach no satisfaction
12. taking sensorial experience as the criterion of faith
13. practically denying the truth of signs: dogmatic terminology refers to no perennial realities, while sacramental acts evoke but don't convey divine grace
14. suppressing or distorting sacred images and downplaying priestly celibacy to placate sinful officials or win their favour.

If any of the stages described sounds disturbingly familiar to us when examining our conscience, let us review our priestly life before it is too late. No matter how gifted and experienced we are, we need the boundaries and certainties which only the Saviour gives us through his Holy Church.

THOMAS MERTON AND PADRE PIO

As a final illustration, the life of Trappist monk Fr Thomas Merton (1915–1968) embodies the modern vulnerability of consecrated men since the end of World War II. Thank God, Fr Merton did not apostatise. But he would have been a real-life equivalent of Fr Rodrigues if the film *Silence* had ended just *before* the fictional Jesuit had made up his mind to trample Christ's picture. These two Western priests were spiritually attracted to Asia, where they both died. Fr Merton went from a sound Catholic doctrine and rule of life to an ever hazier delineation of his faith as his attraction to Buddhism became more explicit. Furthermore, while at the peak of his career as an author, from 1966 to 1967, he admitted to a serious difficulty in keeping his vow of celibacy.[14] His last weeks on earth were spent in India and Thailand in active involvement with pagan Oriental spiritualities and with their religious leaders.[15] The circumstances of Thomas Merton's death near Bangkok on December 10, 1968 were not elucidated.[16] On his last conference in Bangkok, Merton still wore his Cistercian habit, and in his latest writings he referred to Christ as a real Person he loved. It is to be hoped that Fr Merton's faith in Christ and his Church remained unaltered until the end, and his writings and speeches fail to provide ground for formal apostasy. However, the direction he was heading towards was objectively perilous to his soul, as was the

14   His was no isolated case, since Pope Paul VI felt compelled to extol priestly celibacy in his encyclical *Sacerdotalis Caelibatus*, published on June 24, 1967.

15   'Merton spent most of his time on this journey in India, Sri Lanka and Thailand, with brief stops in Hawaii, Tokyo, Hong Kong and Singapore. He planned to meet other monastics, both Christian and Buddhist, to connect with some of the Trappist-Cistercian communities of the region, to investigate possibilities for a new location for a hermitage, to explore more fully Buddhist spiritual practice, and to continue on his own contemplative path. He left San Francisco on October 15, 1968, and, as we know, died in Thailand on December 10–56 days in all.' Donald Grayston, "In the Footsteps of Thomas Merton: Asia," http://merton.org/ITMS/Seasonal/33/33-4Grayston.pdf, accessed 1 June 2020.

16   See Michael Mott's *The Seven Mountains of Thomas Merton* (Boston: Hougton Mifflin Company, 1984), 566–568.

gradual dimming of his orthodoxy to his many readers. Merton's last years are reminiscent of the last days of Fr Rodrigues in the novel *Silence*, released precisely in 1966.[17] Divine Providence mercifully called Fr Merton to judgement earlier in his faith journey than did novelist Shūsaku Endō for his character Fr Rodrigues. While it would be uncharitable to presume that Merton would have ended like Rodrigues, we can learn from the latter's demise and pray for the former's eternal rest.

It pleased the Sovereign High Priest Our Lord to call back to him another well-known priest, only two months and a half before Fr Merton. Fr Pio of Pietrelcina died in Italy on 23rd September 1968, seventy-eight days before Thomas Merton. Both priests were religious, Westerners and internationally famous. They probably knew of each other. St Padre Pio was the first known stigmatist priest, bearing in his flesh the Five Wounds received by the Saviour. Unlike Merton, he wrote no books: the marks in his limbs and side spoke more eloquently than words. In the person of that Capuchin priest, the supremely personal God, our Saviour, gave us the example of a priest visibly configured to him. How comforting to think that St Pio must have prayed from heaven for Thomas Merton, his brother in the priesthood and a fellow-religious, to die in the Lord.

We priests in the twenty-first century know that we are no better, no stronger, no holier than our predecessors. This is why we want to take time to meditate on all these limited protections gradually abandoned or lost by Fr Rodrigues in what we presented earlier as the fourteen stations of priestly apostasy. None of them is decisive when considered separately. But their combination secures our priestly identity, manifesting it to us and to the world. If one of us ever fell—as long as he breathes, he may walk these stations in the reverse order until thorough healing is granted him by the Lord who called us to serve, and by his Mother who adopted us as her sons. She treasures us who are sacramentally configured to her Son Jesus the Sovereign High Priest.

---

17   Merton could not have read the English translation, published soon after his death in 1969.

2

Ordained a Priest in Dachau[1]

The cosmos has fallen into chaos, because Man has given it over to the demons of chaos. And now, our desire is to contemplate Our Lord and have confidence in His eternal Law, so that peace and order may be established amongst us once again and so that mankind will live in a spirit of justice. The Risen Christ will lend us his aid if we pray patiently, if we endure suffering and offer up our sacrifices. And so the spring will re-emerge around us, and the sun will shine through the happiness dwelling once more in our sorely-tested hearts[2].

Karl Leisner was speaking from experience, in this last letter before his liberation from the Nazi concentration camp of Dachau, following six years of detention. Although just thirty years old and ordained a priest only four months earlier, he had developed, through suffering, an understanding of human nature and a spiritual force which make him a model for the priesthood.

We priests cannot help wondering: 'How could he keep hoping amidst such adversity?' Our priestly ministry is not to be compared with Karl's life in Dachau, and few of our priest readers have yet been imprisoned for their faith, thank God. But in our allegedly enlightened, tolerant and democratic 2020s, the world, the flesh and the devil increasingly conspire to undermine our priesthood. We undergo suspicion because of our consecrated celibacy; we

---

1 First published in French in *Sedes Sapientiae* No. 92—translated for *Dowry* magazine, Issue No. 3, Spring 2009 by H. Buttery; revised by A. de Malleray and C. Kingsley-Evans.

2 Karl Leisner quoted by Joachim Schmiedl in *Bienheureux Karl Leisner, jusqu'au bout de l'amour*, (Paris: Pierre Téqui Editeur, 2004), 215.

face opposition for speaking in God's name; and we risk prosecution simply for bearing witness to the natural law. May Blessed Fr Karl's example rekindle our enthusiasm for acting as other Christs, whatever the earthly cost.

KARL'S LIFE

A committed German youth. Karl was born on 28th February 1915 at Rees, in the lower Rhine valley, the first of five children in a strongly Catholic family. When he started at the 'Gymnasium,'[3] he came under the influence of the chaplain, Fr. Walter Vinnenberg, who exercised a remarkable charism for working with young people. When Fr. Vinnenberg left, it seemed obvious that Karl should take his place and so, at the age of sixteen, he was running the Catholic Youth section, first for his region, then for the diocese of Münster.

Answering God's voice rather than Hitler's. It was a retreat at Schoenstatt that led Karl to the decision to become a priest. In the meantime, Adolf Hitler had come to power and young German males were being enlisted for exhausting manual work for the 'Fatherland.' Karl contracted tuberculosis during his 'Service for the Reich' in the marshes of Dahlen. On 1st July 1938, he received the first Minor Orders, and was ordained a Subdeacon[4] on 4th March 1939, then Deacon on 25th March. Tuberculosis was then diagnosed and he was sent to a sanatorium. Hearing of the failed attempt to assassinate Hitler in the Munich beer cellar on 9th November 1939 (the *Führer* had departed earlier than planned), Karl was rash enough to say in front of a colleague: *What a shame that he had already left.* The same day, Karl was denounced, arrested and imprisoned at Fribourg-in-Brisgau. He was not to enjoy freedom again until six long years later.

Sent to concentration camp. Following a spell in the prison hospital at Mannheim, he arrived at the concentration camp of Sachsenhausen on 16th March 1940. Nine months later he was to be found at Dachau, where he stayed from 13th December 1940

---

3 The equivalent of high school.
4 There are four minor orders: Porter, Reader, Exorcist and Acolyte — and four major ones: Subdiaconate, Diaconate, Presbyterate and Episcopate.

until 4th May 1945. His health deteriorated quickly at Dachau, but he continued to comfort those around him in the infirmary and to give support to the dying. His brotherly love and his cheerful, approachable nature won the friendship of his fellow prisoners.

Priest at long last. The 6th September 1944 saw the arrival at Dachau of a very special detainee, His Excellency Gabriel Piguet, Bishop of Clermont-Ferrand in France. It was this bishop who was to ordain Karl a priest in secret on 17th December 1944, with the participation of all the priests held as prisoners. Nine days later, on 26th December 1944, Karl celebrated the Holy Sacrifice of the Mass for the first and last time. Liberated in May 1945, he died in the sanatorium of Planegg on 12th August that year. Pope John-Paul II beatified him on 23rd June 1996, offering him as a model to European youth. Let us now look at certain aspects of the personality of Blessed Karl Leisner.

ALL FOR GOD, BODY AND SOUL

Sensuality. In his private diaries, there are several occasions on which Karl confronts the obstacles that sensuality presents on the pathway to the priesthood. These entries are precious because they demonstrate the triumph of grace in the daily life of a young man no different from anyone else. Faced with the temptations common to boys of his age, Karl fights them with a healthy confidence in divine aid. He writes in 1935, *I set myself the aim this year of respecting the sixth commandment and, as far as I am able with all my weaknesses, to judge, with the grace of God, I have managed to move a fair way along the road.*[5]

Getting married? Furthermore, Karl wondered on various occasions whether he should perhaps marry. At different stages in his life, his great sensitivity and his gentlemanly nature drew him forcefully towards virtuous young ladies, with perhaps a rather idealised perception of Christian marriage, notwithstanding the sanctity of the marital state. The dilemma was most clearly evident with regard to Elisabeth Ruby, the eldest daughter of the

5　Op. cit., p.106.

family with whom Karl was lodging during his year studying at
Fribourg-in-Brisgau. His personal diary is lucid in its description
of the interior struggle experienced as he continued his theological
studies up to the summer of 1938:

> It is as if I no longer knew what is going on inside me.
> A spreading tide and clamour, the happy bubbling over
> of a delicious springtime in the body and in the blood,
> in the mind and in the soul. And yet, oh how hard
> it is to make decisions to take one road rather than
> another in life. Is all to be sacrifice? Can I give up such
> a virtuous, marvellous creature, give up all the joys and
> struggles of a blessed union with a beloved being? [...]
> And yet, everything in me and in her is pushing me
> towards holiness, towards the supreme gift to the Lord.
> Lord, show me the way, and may Your Spirit give a little
> sign to point out the road to follow. I no longer know
> which to choose; I am sick in the depths of my being.[6]

Other saintly young Levites such as St Thomas Aquinas and St
Aloysius Gonzaga seem to have been spared the lure of sensuality
and the overwhelming power of sentimental attraction. Clearly
this was not the case with Karl. His example can encourage so
many young people examining their vocation nowadays, upset
and confused by the ambient eroticism and the preponderance of
emotional discourse in our culture.

PROUD TO BE GERMAN

No less apt as a model is Karl Leisner's filial love for his mother
country. While the tyranny of National Socialism was tightening its
grip on the German people, Karl could clearly see the distinction
between patriotic piety and its corruption by Nazism.

Youth leader. In the context of his responsibilities concerning the organisations for Catholic youth in Münster, Karl had to

6   Op. cit., p.116.

exercise some cunning with the Nazi administration in order to safeguard the independent structure of his groups. This endeavour brought him to a deeper consideration of the fundamental connection between his fidelity to the Catholic Church and his patriotic love for the German people. The two and the love he felt for both, far from being incompatible, were complementary and mutually enriching indeed:

> I must lead German youth! So I must throw off all gloomy thoughts and turn towards the motherland! I must be ready to offer my life! My task is to lead Catholic youth towards the German nation, and to build the German nation out of holy Catholic youth! I feel the deepest love and attachment for the German people, and I want to do this: I want to forget all the bad things, think positively and get to work! The German people must become once again a Christian people, a Catholic people, as in the days of the German Empire, its people and its land. So let us scale the ramparts with our heads held high, our faces turned towards freedom and honesty! St Michael, be my help, my holy patron and protector, St George, my model of gallantry, and Holy Mother of God, use your power to intercede for me and use me as you and your Son wish in the holy mission amongst the German people! My people, here is my hand in an eternal embrace! My country, here is my heart, which, full of love, was looking for you and for my Nation [...]. Forward, let us act like Catholics and Germans! With You, my Lord and my God! For nothing has any power, nothing can exist, without You![7]

Prophetic eloquence. Had they been written in less disturbing times, these lines might seem simply bombastic, expressing the ardour of a romantic young Christian. But Karl wrote them in

7 Op. cit., p.96.

1934 when he had been appointed by Bishop von Galen[8] to lead the *Jungschar* (the diocesan youth movement), one year after the election of Adolf Hitler. In these days of the *Hitlerjugend*, of torch-light processions in the Nuremberg stadium stirring up German youth, a young 'Aryan' needed a great deal of clear-headedness and courage in order to claim that his Catholicism (and not the official neo-paganism) was the best means of expressing his patriotism. These, of course, are only words: but ten years later, Karl was to risk his life for the cause of bringing his country back to Christ. While the political horizon was darkening in Germany, the young leader of the *Jungschar* was quite correctly adopting a prophetic style: *My people, here is my hand in an eternal embrace!*

New world order. Today, both patriotism and religion are regarded with suspicion. To love one's country and want to defend it, or to cherish Catholicism and to try to speak up for it, are seen by our politically-correct censors as evidence of living in the past and being intolerant. The arrival of a new world order and that of a universal syncretism require the eradication of national identity and of religious denominations. Neither a reactionary nor a zealot, Karl Leisner kept in mind that all truly human activities have as their aim the service of God. This, in turn, is made possible chiefly by adhering to the true Faith, according to the circumstances in different cultural milieux and countries at various times.

OFFERING UP HIS SUFFERINGS

Karl's tuberculosis was diagnosed in May 1939. His imprisonment also began that year, and continued until three months before his death in the sanatorium of Planegg in August 1945. Even though the prison conditions had varied, ranging from the individual cell at the beginning to the communal huts of Dachau, their increasing severity had evidently aggravated the illness. Some prison doctors may have intended to make their patients well, but their

---

8   Clemens August Graf von Galen (1878–1946), later Cardinal, was beatified on 9 October 2005. A heroic defender of the natural and divine laws against the Nazis, he was nicknamed 'The Lion of Münster.'

efforts were paralysed by the growing shortage of medication as the defeats of the *Reich* continued.

Aching body. Karl experienced a great deal of physical suffering, both from the tuberculosis in his lungs and from the endless mal-treatment meted out to him as to all the prisoners: *At about 4:30am we would arrive at the chapel for Mass. Afterwards we would go to the parade ground for roll call, wearing thin work clothes, even in winter, with wooden clogs on our feet. The last ones to arrive at the parade ground would be severely beaten as they made their way there. The guards treated them so badly that several later died prematurely.*[9]

'Traitor.' The damage done to morale must have been at least as painful. Karl, who had seen German youth coming into bloom and striving for the reign of Christ, now saw it corrupted by Nazism and wasted in bloody combat on the ever increasing battle fronts, for the glory of the infallible *Führer*. It hurt Karl to be seen as a traitor to his country when in fact he was burning with love for it and for its citizens. He also suffered the anxiety of knowing that reprisals might be taken against his family, of whom he had very little news.

Ever to be ordained? A yet more personal sacrifice was surely weighing on his soul: that of seeing his chances of being ordained as a priest slipping further away each day. As a single man, he had sacrificed his genuine inclinations towards marriage in order to give himself totally to Christ; as a seminarian, he had *de facto* given up any possibility of devoting his organisational skills and his charism to the cause of resistance against the Nazi oppressor. But it would take him several months to prepare for priestly ordination under normal conditions. Ordained a deacon on 25th March 1939, he learned two months later that he had tuberculosis: this would jeopardise his progression towards the priesthood. Arrested five months later, he realised that his chances of soon becoming a priest were dwindling further still. After several years of detention without any great hope of being released or even of surviving, the young Deacon Leisner was constrained by circumstances to place

9   Op. cit., p.176.

his priestly ordination well and truly in the hands of Christ: *It is
now five and a half years since I became a deacon. My whole being
is yearning and praying to enter into the priesthood.*[10] In the face
of this extreme difficulty, it became apparent that only God, the
Author of every vocation, could ensure that this prisoner suffering
from tuberculosis would one day go up to the altar.

Peaceful hope. During his last months in the camp, when he
did not know whether his ruined health would ever allow him to
exercise priestly functions, Karl displayed a surprising and wholly
supernatural confidence in divine Providence:

> What do we have to worry about? All will be well. This
> is God's way of watching over me and I want to show
> my gratitude towards him and continue to accept my
> situation with calmness and patience. It is precisely the
> mysteries of Lent and of Easter which lift us up from our
> grey and sombre daily lives, up to the heavenly realities
> and give us that last ounce of strength with which to
> overcome all that weighs us down on this dust-covered
> Earth, so that we may always keep our gaze fixed on
> the eternal stars, despite our transient burdens.[11]

This is no blind optimism, but a profound theological hope
which, far from dodging the trials at issue, rather swallows them
up and feeds on them in order to allow the soul to grow in grace.
All those who suffer, fellow-clerics in particular, will draw strength
from these lines because their author, familiar with helplessness,
experienced the reality of divine assistance. Deacon Leisner may
never have sang the Gospel from an *evangeliarum* at high Mass,
and yet he advances to us the Good News through his witness,
shining like a medieval Gospel cover case embellished with gleam-
ing gemstones (the bloodclots of his wrecked lungs) set in precious
metal (the twisted steel of the Dachau barbed wire).

10   Op. cit., p. 202.
11   Op. cit., p.214.

A PRIEST FOREVER

Hatred for Christ. The Nazi leaders wanted to eradicate Christianity altogether and replace it with some 'religion' based on race and adapted to their objectives. They thought they would be able to smother the Protestant and Catholic Churches relatively quickly. Their plan was hatched at meetings between the Nazi chiefs whom Hitler trusted most: Goering, Goebbels, Rosenberg, Hess, Schemm and Von Schirach. Those who were less virulent in their opposition to religion, like Von Epp and Von Papen were probably not informed of the plan. Hitler wanted to start by manipulating the Churches, judging that their conservative nature would incline them to lend support for the *fatherland* and to oppose Communism.[12] But he was also aware that the Churches would not approve of racism, war and subservience to the State, and he prepared to destroy them later. 2,579 Catholic priests were deported to Dachau alone and 1,034 of them died there, making this camp in Bavaria probably the largest priests' cemetery in the world. Numerous 'survivors' died shortly afterwards from the effects of their deportation, like Karl Leisner.

French Bishop prisoner. On 6th September 1944, His Excellency Gabriel Piguet, Bishop of Clermont-Ferrand, arrived to swell the ranks of the Catholic clergy deported to Dachau. For Karl, and for those who were supporting him in his vocation, this was a glimmer of hope. Bishop Piguet agreed to ordain Karl in secret if Bishop von Galen (the Bishop of Münster, Karl's diocese) and the Archbishop of Münich (the diocese covering Dachau) gave permission as required by canon law. On 29th October 1944, the "Lion of Münster," Blessed Clemens August von Galen, wrote to Karl: (...) *I very gladly give you my permission for the sacrament to be conferred there. The only condition is that the ordination be valid, and that this can be proved afterwards. May God give you his blessing!*[13]

---

12 That is, only after 22nd June, 1941, when Hitler chose to end his secret alliance with the Soviets, his formal accomplices since 23rd August, 1939, when J. von Ribbentrop and V. Molotov, the foreign ministers of the German Reich and of USSR, had signed in Moscow the Treaty of Non-aggression.

13 Op. cit., p. 203.

Ecumenical endeavour. A great number of clergy and lay people, Catholics and Protestants, took enormous risks by meeting together and making the liturgical *regalia* necessary for the ordination: putting together makeshift episcopal ornaments, including the mitre, gloves, stockings, chasuble, ring and crozier; as well as the priestly vestments which Karl was to wear; and smuggling into the camp the Holy Oils for anointing the hands of the ordinand. Several such items may still be seen in the display cases of the Carmel at Dachau, situated on the edge of the camp. An improvised monstrance is strangely reminiscent of the one displayed at the memorial of Les Lucs-sur-Boulogne in the Vendée (France), which bears witness to Catholic resistance in another instance of oppression. One can also see tabernacle doors made of beaten tin-plate, recycled no doubt from food tins; episcopal stockings made of mattress covers... The obvious care taken by the prisoners in the creation of these objects is very touching and offers an antidote to liturgical minimalism when we remember the lack of time, materials and strength available to the prisoners when making these objects, while risking their lives in the process: *A Russian prisoner made a ring for the bishop, a German Benedictine made a crozier bearing the name of Karl Leisner's group in Schönstatt, Victor in vinculis. The violet cassock and the mozzetta were put together using leftovers from Nazi pillages in the Warsaw Ghetto. An English oblate Father made a mitre in silk and pearls.*[14]

First Holy Mass. The young German Karl Leisner was secretly ordained on 17th December 1944 by a French bishop, his fellow-deportee, surrounded by German and Polish priests. His first Holy Mass was celebrated on the day after Christmas 1944, the feast of Saint Stephen, deacon and martyr, in the chapel of the priests' block in Dachau. Tuberculosis, aggravated by maltreatment, prevented Karl from offering the Holy Sacrifice again before he appeared before the Sovereign Priest Jesus Christ eight months later.

Wasted? On a human scale, we could deplore the disproportion between the years Karl spent preparing—through study and then

14 Op. cit., p. 204.

through suffering, culminating in this clandestine ordination — and the pathetic brevity of his priestly ministry. Divine Providence reminds us through Karl's fate that the priesthood is first and foremost a sacramental identification with Christ the Mediator and Intercessor. The apostolate radiates out from this configuration of the soul of the priest, marked by the sacerdotal character, with his divine Model. Even though he only offered Holy Mass once, Father Leisner fulfilled his priestly function completely. In this application of the merits of Christ for the Redemption of mankind, Karl undoubtedly offered his many years of suffering and prayer, through which God had prepared him to act in His Name and Person. The Sacrifice which Karl offered sacramentally only once had been offered each day in his person, as he accepted his deportation and lived it out in such a Christian manner.

To Fellow-Priests and Young People. Whether they are good or bad, examples do influence us. Karl Leisner, who was beatified by Pope John Paul II on 23rd June 1996 in the Berlin Olympic stadium, set an example which encourages us in several ways. He suffered martyrdom in the modern era, at the hands of neo-pagan totalitarianism but in a European country which had long been Christian. Several decades later, his heroic witness to truth in charity inspires us.

True peace. Now, we know that peace is fragile and does not consist simply of the absence of cannon fire. Other wars are raging today, against unborn children and against the purity of those who survive, against the stability of families and against the very survival of those who are ill or old in hospitals: *Once the law is trampled on, once injustice comes to power, peace becomes threatened, or worse, is already destroyed.*[15] Young priests and laity will play a vital role in determining the outcome of these conflicts which are more spiritual than political, but no less destructive than the war of 1939–45. Following in the footsteps of Karl Leisner, although confronted with a hostility which is for the moment more subdued

15   Cardinal Joseph Ratzinger, *L'Europe, ses fondements, aujourd'hui et demain*, (St-Maurice: Editions Saint-Augustin, 2005), 101.

than that of Dachau, priests and young people are called to stand up for the respect due to every innocent human life and for the supernatural vocation of every soul. Karl Leisner's life shows that fidelity to Christ is the principle which allows us to live our lives with confidence, transforming our trials into a series of steps leading to our deeper union with God.

The past remembered for a safer future. Films about the failed assassination attempt of Adolf Hitler by the Catholic Colonel Claus von Stauffenberg, or about the 'White Rose' Christian youth resistance to Hitler have provided some reminders about Nazi totalitarianism in history. It is good to keep the memory intact and updated so as to prevent the return of oppression. But that requires that all the factors be identified. With this in mind, how can we not deplore the terrible weakness which allowed Stalin's army to be included in the group of liberators? For half of Europe, in the East, 1945 marked the shift to yet another tyranny organised to last for decades. How many soldiers and workmen, how many Polish, Czech and Hungarian priests who had survived the Nazi camps, were simply transferred to Soviet gulags? As for the Iron Curtain, it was not put in place in order to prevent the westerners from coming in to enjoy Communist 'freedom.' Sadly, as warned by Our Lady at Fatima, Communism subsequently spread to many countries, and culturally to the West where its grip is tightening.

The Truth shall set us free. The true liberation of Europe did not take place until the fall of that shameful Wall, an event in which a most famous Pole, Pope John Paul II, played a decisive role. It is significant that his successor to the See of Peter was a German who, as a young seminarian, also suffered from Nazi coercion. At a time when Europe is searching for her soul, this papal transition illustrated the Church's capacity to overcome antagonisms, and her unifying mission.

In his address to the young people of Strasbourg on 8th October 1996, Pope John Paul II said:

> Many young people have borne witness to this sort of sacrifice to Christ. I am thinking especially of Marcel

Callo. I am also thinking of the young German, Karl Leisner who, before being sent to the concentration camp at Dachau, wrote: 'The secret of Europe's strength is Christ.'[16]

Needless to say, this statement applies to non-European countries as well. May we priests help inspire very large numbers of young men and young women in Europe and throughout the world to answer the call of the Church. May they enter the lists and line up with resolution and serenity under the banner of Our Lady and of her divine Son Jesus Christ.

16   Op. cit., p.241.

3

Handling The Right Body[1]

THIS BODY WHICH IS HIS.... WHAT BODY DOES
Pope St Pius X refer to here in his exhortation to Catholic priests,[2]
exactly 110 years before the revelations on clerical sex abuse in summer 2018? Is it the *Eucharistic* Body of Christ, that is, the sacred
Host? No. Is it the *Mystical* Body of Christ, the gathering of the
faithful as one Church? Neither. What is meant in this instance is
the physical body of the priest himself, with his lips, tongue and
hands. This is what Pope St Pius X, arguably the greatest pope in
modern times, calls *This body which is His . . .* —Christ's own Body.
Rediscovering the meaning of such physical appropriation of the
priest by Christ is essential, we suggest, to understand the present
crisis, heal the wounds incurred and obtain superabundant graces.

The Church is still reeling following revelations of sexual abuse
on an unprecedented scale. It was perpetrated by numerous priests,
by bishops and even by a cardinal, over decades and against hundreds of victims, not only in America but also in Europe and on
other continents. Sexual abuse is a crime. It is also a grave scandal
when it stains the Christian name. Of all Christians, when those
appointed pastors of souls betray their mission to such an extent,
the harm is even greater.

Most of the crimes uncovered occurred over the past fifty years,
were against young men. We ask ourselves how so many priests
since the late 1960s, have indulged in the vice of ephebophilia, or
'lust for young men.' (*Ephebophilia* pertains to homosexuality as
distinct from sexual attraction to children, known as *paedophilia*.)
How can a man, consecrated to God in the most solemn and
public manner according to Catholic doctrine, break his vow of

---

1   This article was first published in *Dowry* No. 40, Winter 2018.
2   Cf. *Haerent Animo* Part I, St. Pius X, 4th August 1908.

chastity, with the aggravating circumstances of acting 1) against nature (the victim is his own sex) and 2) against his mission (as a trusted protector rather than a predator)?

ABSTINENT FOR GOD'S SAKE

These abusive clerics were consecrated body and soul to God, so as to consecrate the Body and Blood of God made Man, Jesus Christ, in the Most Holy Eucharist. According to the traditional discipline prevailing in the Western Church, (and in the Eastern Churches, at least for bishops) they had committed themselves to celibacy. They had renounced the goods of marriage and family so as to be integrally configured to Christ the Sovereign High Priest, celibate and Spouse to his mystical Bride the Church. But after a while, if not from the start, they craved other bodies. They lusted after human flesh.

The fact that their victims were of the same sex is an aggravating circumstance. But it should be borne in mind that *any* deliberate sexual activity would have been a betrayal of their commitment to chastity. In fact, it is timely to observe that sexual activity is fully legitimate for *any* man and woman *only* when open to procreation with the view to raising children as saints, which only Christian marriage fully guarantees. Put simply, the purpose of sex is to form families, not to gratify self or partners. Sex is given to increase the number of the elect through building up domestic churches. Sex is for pro-creating new rational human beings to worship the Most Holy Trinity for eternity. The Creator of the human race embedded sexual pleasure in the marital act as a generous incentive for the pro-creation of more human worshippers. By divine ordinance, the marital act is like a plane bound for blissful eternity. Lust in every form hijacks it.

SPIRITUAL FATHERHOOD

Priests pursue the noble procreative end through spiritual father-hood, begetting a soul to divine grace through holy Baptism, nour-ishing it through Holy Communion, and fostering it through the other sacraments, sacred actions and Church teaching. Priests are not angels, though. They are men of flesh and blood. Like any man (or woman) they rely on divine grace to master their sexual desires and channel them according to God's law of life. For celibate clergy, this means offering up sexual pleasure as a sacrifice to God, affirming the reality of the invisible fecundity embedded in them by God at their ordination through the sacramental character of the priesthood. Spiritual fatherhood is no mere substitute for biological fatherhood, a consolation prize. Rather, it expresses the essence of the divine fatherhood, imaging *the Father of our Lord Jesus Christ, of whom all paternity in heaven and earth is named* (Eph 3:14-15).

The divine powers granted to the priest are objective and permanent. They remain, even though their use might be hindered through sickness or imprisonment; even though the clerical state might be lost; and regardless of the priest's personal merits or demerits. These powers essentially consist in making Christ present under the externals of bread and wine at Holy Mass, and in absolving souls from their sins in Confession. The more one believes these truths, the more one will value priestly celibacy. Why? Because priestly celibacy points to the reality of Christ's saving presence in the sacraments of the Church. Fallen men hold sexual activity as a fundamental 'need.' 'We cannot do,' they think, 'without a body to hold.' The celibate priesthood does not frustrate this aspiration — it elevates it. Priestly celibacy implies that the Eucharistic Body of Christ is real enough to reward man's chastity. Priestly celibacy suggests that absolving penitents is a genuine outpouring of divine life throughout the mystical Body of Christ, his Church.

HABEAS CORPUS

Thus, faith in and love for the Eucharistic Body of Christ, and for his Mystical Body the Church, should grow in inverse proportion with lust for human bodies. The priests and bishops who committed sexual abuse got hold of the *wrong* body. Neglecting the Saviour's Body, they craved the creatures' bodies, and clung to them. As a comparison, they are like a state officer hearing the words *Habeas Corpus,* without listening further. *Habeas Corpus* is the fourteenth century English law stating that a person can only be kept in prison following a court's decision. Instead of hearing: 'By what right do you hold this body?' — clerical abusers wrongly understand *Habeas Corpus* as: 'You should have the body — and keep it!'

To keep the body? They did receive such a mandate though, at their ordination. They were once appointed 'keepers of the Body.' On that most solemn occasion, kneeling before the bishop, their hands touching the chalice containing wine and the host on the paten, they were told: *Receive the power to offer sacrifice to God, and to celebrate Masses for the living and the dead, in the name of the Lord.* Priests are entrusted with the Lord's Eucharistic Body (and Precious Blood), for the benefit of the Lord's Mystical Body (his Church). Thus, the problem is not for celibate clerics to handle Someone else's Body, but to handle the wrong body. Priests have a right to a Body — with a capital B.

AIMING FOR GOD'S BODY

Significantly, handling God's Body requires purity of mind and body for priests. As the bishop admonishes them: *Be holy as you deal with holy things. When you celebrate the mystery of the Lord's death, see to it that by mortifying your bodies you rid yourselves of all vice and concupiscence.* Thus does Holy Mother Church remind her priests when, vesting for Holy Mass daily, she teaches them to recite the following prayer as they tie the cincture around their waist, over the alb: *Gird me, O Lord, with the cincture of purity, and quench in my loins the fire of concupiscence, that the virtue of continence and chastity may abide in me.* A mysterious exchange is happening between one body and another. The priest renounces access to any created body, thus mortifying his own body, so as to handle Christ's Eucharistic Body and feed It to Christ's Mystical Body, the Church.

A similar swap occurs in Holy Matrimony according to traditional Church teaching. The Code of Canon Law written under Pope St Pius X described matrimonial consent as an act of the will *by which each party gives and accepts a perpetual and exclusive right over the body (of the spouse), for acts which are of themselves suitable for the generation of children* (c. 1081, § 2). Matrimonial consent involves a transfer of rights: the object of consent is the handing over of an essential right — the *ius in corpus,* or 'right over the body.'

Could this shed light on the priestly state and prerogative, analogically? A consecrated celibate and a bishop, St Paul wrote: *With Christ I am nailed to the cross. I live, now not I; but Christ liveth in me. And that I live now in the flesh: I live in the faith of the Son of God* (Gal 2:19-20). Here, we see how sacrificial union between Christ and his ordained minister produces an existential exchange, whereby Christ lives in his priest, and the priest in Christ. Generally speaking, this applies to any Christian, since we are all called to surrender body and soul to Christ, that God may dwell in us as in his temple: *...reckon that you are dead to sin, but alive unto God, in Christ Jesus our Lord. Let no sin therefore reign in your mortal body, so as to obey the lusts thereof* (Rom 6:11-12). But it applies more fully to priests, by virtue of the priestly character.

A LOVING EXCHANGE

The divine powers to transubstantiate matter and absolve souls are embedded in the priest, and only in the priest, at his ordination. These powers remain forever, even after death. Such abiding divine capacity is activated every time the priest knowingly and willingly acts *in persona Christi,* e.g. when praying, blessing and teaching. This activation is never greater than during Holy Mass. When at Consecration the priest — let's call him 'Fr Jim' — says: 'This is *my* body,' the word 'my' essentially refers to Christ, not to Fr Jim's body. And yet, the words are uttered, physically, through Fr Jim's mouth, and intellectually understood by Fr Jim's brain, and willed by him at the same time. Simultaneously, in Fr Jim's hands, the bread becomes Christ's Body. In other words, an existential swap occurs, whereby Fr Jim surrenders his body (and soul) to Christ, so that Christ might now lie in Fr Jim's hands. Christ receives Fr Jim's body through appropriation; Fr Jim receives Christ's Body through transubstantiation. The consecrated Host is the Eucharistic Body of Christ, because Fr Jim's body has become the 'ministerial' Body of Christ.

The word 'ministerial' here does not mean a temporary Church function, however helpful, like being appointed sacristan or collection counter for a year. Rather, only a priest's body can be termed Christ's 'ministerial' Body, by virtue of the ontological modification which the priest undergoes at ordination, when the priestly character embeds in him divine powers forever. What encouragement for priests to realize that their body (as animated by a soul) is not theirs anymore, but Christ's. When rising in the morning and shaving, when eating his breakfast, when cycling to visit his flock or for leisure, as well as on any other occasion, the priest can think of his body as Christ's ministerial body.

All whatsoever you do in word or in work, do all in the name of the Lord Jesus Christ, giving thanks to God and the Father by him (Col 3:17). This lofty call to every Christian is fulfilled in the priest not only spiritually but ontologically, every time he acts *in persona Christi*, and supremely during Holy Mass, at Consecration. Then, the *ius in corpus* essential to the sacrament of Holy Matrimony is activated, analogically, when the priest surrenders his body to Christ, for Christ's words to make his Body present in the hands of his priest.

TO GIVE THE SACRED

Notably, as for Christian spouses, this exchange of rights over each other's body is meant to benefit *others*, namely, the family. By its very nature, Eucharistic Consecration is not a private prayer or initiative of the priest, but a cultic glorification of God and a public service to all the faithful, within and without the pews, alive and deceased. At the same time, the sacramental intimacy between the priest and Christ the Sovereign High Priest is traditionally secured during the Consecration through the use of low voice rather than loud speaking, and through the priest's posture. The congregation kneeling behind him, the priest whispers the sacred formulas while his elbows rest upon the altar, the tabernacle and altar card in front of him screening off the corporal and the gifts during the double transubstantiation.

This intimacy is by no means selfish. It is ordered to the service of the flock. Immediately after the Consecration (and his first genuflection), the priest rises and elevates the Sacred Body for the congregation to see and adore. Soon after, he will feed the people with the immaculate flesh of the Lamb of God. The etymology of the word 'sacerdotal,' i.e. 'priestly,' is *sacer-dos*, or to 'give the sacred.' Thus, there is essential continuity between Consecration and Communion. The same *sacer-dos*, that is, the priest, makes Christ present upon the altar, and communicates him to the people.

Because we cannot love what we don't know, understanding better the faith of the Church about the Eucharistic sacrifice and presence, as well as about the ministerial priesthood, is a powerful incentive to clerical morality. This requires the teaching of sound philosophy and theology at the seminary, as well as respect for the letter and the spirit of the Eucharistic Liturgy. The more a priest understands the reality of his sacramental configuration to Christ, setting him apart from other baptised people to present their petitions to God and to channel to them the life of grace, the safer his soul will be, and those of the flock.

Intellectual persuasion does not suffice though. It must flower into moments of daily intimacy with Christ in prayer, and in a devout offering of Holy Mass. In that respect, priests should be encouraged to offer Holy Mass daily, even without fellow-priests concelebrating. Often, while on pilgrimage or on holiday, priests are denied the right to offer Holy Mass individually. This contradicts the law of the Church stating that: *Each priest shall always retain his right to celebrate Mass individually....* [3] As those 'giving the sacred,' priests should also use their anointed hands to communicate Christ's Body to the faithful: *Extraordinary ministers may distribute Holy Communion at Eucharistic celebrations only when there are no ordained ministers present....* [4] Recalling Pope St Pius X's words: *This body which is his...*, the priest will know

---

3   Vatican II, *Sacrosanctum Concilium* 57,2.

4   Cf. Instruction On Certain Questions Regarding the Collaboration of the Non-Ordained Faithful In the Sacred Ministry As Priest, Article 8 § 2–15th August 1997.

himself to be Christ's in a real, physical sense. He will give thanks for such intimacy, as fecund as it is chaste. In Holy Communion, lending his limbs as Christ's ministerial Body, the priest will give the Eucharistic Body of Christ to his Mystical Body, the Church — a sacramental fulfilment of the doxology at Mass: *through Him, with Him and in Him*. . . .

May the Virgin Mother of God, Mother of priests, St John Mary Vianney and St Pio of Pietrelcina intercede for all priests.

4

In Persona Christi

THE PRIEST OFFERING THE HOLY SACRIFICE OF
the Mass is said to act *in persona Christi*, that is, 'in the person
of Christ.' What is the meaning of that expression used, among
others, by St Thomas Aquinas quoting St Paul: *for your sake, in the
person of Christ?*[1] To understand it, we need to call to mind what
the Church teaches about the Person of Christ. These dogmatic
pronouncements are supported by the philosophical definition of
personhood. We will thus examine the following topics:

1. What the person of Christ is. Divine persons are fulfilled,
not hindered, through mutual interaction. So it must be also for
human persons, as exemplified by Christ's humanity. The three
sacramental characters configure humans to Christ, and supremely
the priestly character.

2. The ancient masks of Greek actors provide an etymological
illustration of the concept of person. Christ's human nature can
be seen as the 'persona' of the Word Eternal. Priests are 'personas'
of Christ.

3. Martyrdom is the ultimate identification with Christ. Martyrs
bear witness to the triple unity of the human person, of society
and of Christ. This is supremely the case for priests martyred in
connection with the Holy Eucharist.

4. Mental prayer as union with Christ. No priest can fall gravely
if he prays. Catholic contemplation fulfils the priest. But if other
types of meditation cancel personhood, they threaten prayer life
and undermine our union with Christ.

5. Relating to invisible persons. A genuine relationship with the
three divine Persons and with Christ in particular must lead to

1   Cf. *Summa* IIIa Q22 a4, quoting 2 Cor 2:10: *propter vos, in persona
Christi.*

relating to other non-visible persons. These fall into five categories: the holy angels (and the fallen ones); Our Lady and the saints; the Eucharistic Lord; the Holy Souls in Purgatory; the unborn.

6. The Blessed Virgin Mary configures the priests to her Son Jesus. The seven vesting prayers before Holy Mass are like a liturgical Incarnation. This summarizes the process of priestly formation during which seven orders are imparted to the seminarian over seven years. The daily vesting of the priest refers to obedience, poverty and chastity.

THE PERSON OF CHRIST AND OUR PERSON

What is the Person of Christ? A person is a being endowed with reason and free will. This defines persons created and uncreated, visible and invisible. The person of Christ is God the Word Eternal, Second Person of the Holy Trinity. As such, the person of Christ is uncreated and invisible. The person of Christ is not human. It is divine. But this divine person has assumed the human nature with all its physical and spiritual components, namely, a body with limbs and organs, and a soul with faculties. There are not two persons in Christ however, one human and one divine. On the contrary, there are two natures in Christ: the human nature and the divine nature. But these two natures are united (not merged) under one single self which is divine. When with his human lips and mouth Christ says 'I,' the person referred to is God the Son, Second Person of the Holy Trinity.

Humans are meant to reflect Christ. In the visible world, man is the only creature made after the image and likeness of God.[2] But the essence of an image is to refer to its original. The more faithfully an image evokes its original, the better it is. Thus, humans are fulfilled inasmuch as they reflect God. How do we reflect God? We do not reflect God through our bodily configuration, since

2   CCC 355 "God created man in his own image, in the image of God he created him, male and female he created them." Man occupies a unique place in creation: (I) he is "in the image of God"; (II) in his own nature he unites the spiritual and material worlds; (III) he is created "male and female"; (IV) God established him in his friendship.

God as a pure spirit has no flesh. What is spiritual in us is our soul, the form[3] of our body. Our soul endowed with reason and free will is what makes us alike to God. Hence, we reflect God inasmuch as our mind knows God as perfect truth and our will desires God as supreme good.

No person is independent. Existing in relation to another than us — namely God — is not accidental or detrimental to us humans. On the contrary, it is essential to us. Because we were created by God, we are related to him in a subordinated way. But because we are proud (having lost original humility), we find it debasing to be relative to someone else, even to God. What we readily accept is to see other persons as relative to us, because it glorifies us. On the contrary, admitting that we are relative to other persons repels us. We mistakenly seek autonomy to affirm our identity, when correlation is what fulfils us by nature.

The Holy Trinity is personal interaction. Such a truth is revealed to us in the very essence of God as Trinity. God is the source of all being and the One whose perfection we reflect, albeit in a limited way. How telling then to realise that God's inner life essentially is relationality. Indeed, the three divine Persons are relative to each other. Because all three are divine, they are equal. Thus, their mutual relationality entails no subordination, no greater or lesser rank. In fact, the three divine Persons are subsisting relations: God the Father is fatherhood itself, God the Son is sonship itself, and God the Holy Ghost is procession itself. The mystery of the Holy Trinity shows that being relative to another is not demeaning. On the contrary, in God, being, and being related to, is one and the same thing.

---

3   As the form of our body, our soul is coextensive to it. There is no organ, no limb, no atom of our body which is not shaped by our soul and constantly animated by it. This shows the dignity of our body. Far from being an impersonal vehicle for our soul, or even worse, a prison for our soul, our body reflects God's splendour inasmuch as it is animated by our immortal soul, substantially united with it. Consequently, we cease to exist as a person as long as our soul is separated from our body, namely, between death and the resurrection of the body. Finally, the fact that in Jesus Christ God assumed our human nature body and soul proves that our bodily condition is good and even appropriate to the divinity.

Relationality among creatures. Unsurprisingly the holy angels, as the persons closer to God by nature, imitate this essential feature of the divine persons. Indeed the word 'angel' means 'messenger.' Transmitting a message implies a fundamental ordering of self to a recipient on behalf of a sender. As God's messengers to men, angels are by essence relational. The nine angelical choirs radiate the divine mystery of personal relatedness. The names of the three angels known to us express this with the Hebrew suffix -*el* which indicates their relation to God on behalf of men. Thus 'Michael' means 'Who [i.e. no one] is alike to God!' 'Raphael' means 'God heals.' 'Gabriel' means 'Power of God.' On the contrary, to interrupt a relationship means to *interfere*, literally: to *throw across*, of which the Greek equivalent is *dia-bolos*, the etymology for the English word *devil*. Thus, some angels fell precisely in so far as they refused to be relative to God and to whoever God would send them to as his messengers. How telling then that the person closer to God by grace, the Immaculate Virgin Mary, as soon as having become God's Mother following the embassy of the Archangel Gabriel, would set up in haste to assist her cousin Elizabeth in her pregnancy. No sooner did Our Lady conceive God in her virginal womb that she showed herself as relative to another, namely, the Precursor and his mother. On the contrary, thirty years later another virgin named Salome interfered quite literally when asking for the head of the Baptist, who stood as a witness to a treasured relation, the valid marriage of her mother with Herod's brother Philip. Indeed, martyrs are among humans the closest equivalent to the (good) angels, since the word *martyr* means *witness*, i.e. a person entirely relative to the person of Christ the Saviour.

Schesiphobia **is a consequence of sin.** We sinners pathologically project a demeaning shadow on the notion of relation. We do this because of our pride, inherited through the original sin. We fallen men spontaneously see other persons either as rivals, or as oppressors, or as commodities. We think a relationship is a hindrance or a convenience, rather than the condition for our personal fulfilment. But this twisted perception is accidental to our human nature, which is essentially relational as we have said, reflecting our divine origin. Let us make use of a neologism to illustrate this point. The Greek word for 'relation' is 'schésī' (σχέση). We all suffer from 'schesiphobia,' namely, an irrational aversion to being relative to someone else. Divine grace heals us from this fear of being relative. The saints are those men, women and children who discover that being relative to God fulfils them. They are not 'schesi-phobic,' but 'schesiphile.' The saints experience and demonstrate that being relative to God refines, enhances and consecrates their uniqueness, instead of undermining it. The saints welcome with awesome gratitude their relational identity as children to God the Father, as brethren to fellow men for the love of God, as stewards to God's material creation and as pupils to the angels our guardians.

The humanity of Jesus is relative to his divinity. In the Lord Jesus Christ, the human nature is restored and elevated to a dignity far beyond its original condition. And yet, the human body and soul of Jesus are united not under a human self, but under a divine self, namely, the uncreated Person of God the Son. Never more than in Our Lord was the human nature relative to God; never was it more elevated as well. The human body and soul of Jesus Christ not only refer to God the Son, but they literally and immediately *are* his. In Our Lord, humanity is the conjoined instrument of the divinity. 'That a human nature should not possess its own connatural human personality is a fact which transcends the order of nature; that upon this humanity should be bestowed a divine Personality is a sublime and ineffable condescension of God to our race.'[4]

Divine relativeness perfects human nature. In Our Lord Jesus Christ, the perfect man, we contemplate our human nature as supremely glorified *because* radically relative to God. Whereas our pride opposes relationality and perfection, the example of Christ shows us that perfection increases with relationality. Numerous times, Our Lord stresses his relationality to his heavenly Father: *I came down from heaven, not to do my own will, but the will of him that sent me* (Jn 6:38). Doing the Father's will is to Our Lord

4 Cf. *The Teaching of the Catholic Church*, Rev George D. Smith, Essay XI, Jesus Christ, God and Man, p. 378. (London: Burns & Oates, 1952).

more than compliance. Rather, it is his very sustenance: *Jesus saith to them, "My meat is to do the will of him that sent me, that I may perfect his work"* (Jn 4:34). The Saviour embraces what our human nature spontaneously abhors, namely, suffering, as the most eloquent proof of his submission to his Father's will: *he fell upon his face, praying, and saying: "My Father, if it be possible, let this chalice pass from me. Nevertheless not as I will, but as thou wilt"* (Mt 26:39).

Men's redemption implies imitating Christ's humanity. We are called to imitate Our Blessed Lord. The imitation of Christ was beautifully explained by Thomas a Kempis in his classical masterpiece by the same title, composed c. 1418–1427. The imitation of Christ is also called the *sequela Christi*, a Latin expression meaning 'following Christ.' What is meant by imitation or following of Christ? No literal imitation is expected of us, but a spiritual one. For example, we need not work for thirty years in a carpenter's shop. Nor would riding a donkey guarantee our sanctification. And dying on a cross may be far beyond what we can bear. But doing the Father's will in our everyday circumstances, such is the constant and safe imitation of Christ. We can do this inasmuch as we let ourselves be prompted and guided by the very Spirit of Jesus Christ, namely, the Holy Ghost. Such is the beautiful process of our being shaped into Christ or 'christiformed,' to quote fifteenth century theologian Nicholas of Cusa (1401–1464) in his Brixen sermons: *Thus, when the Spirit of Jesus is sent into a human soul, it shapes it after Christ, as its virtues and operations truly demonstrate. "By their fruits you shall know them": if a man's works have the shape of Christ, he also must be in the shape of Christ.*[5]

Sacramental configuration to Christ. The Lord Jesus instituted the seven sacraments to make our souls like his. Three sacraments imprint the indelible seal of Christ in the soul: Holy Baptism, Confirmation and the Priesthood or Holy Orders. Through Holy

5   *Sic dum spiritus Iesu immittitur in animam humanam, facit ipsam christiformem, et virtus atque operatio ipsius hoc verum ostendunt. A fructibus eorum enim cognoscetis eos; quando opera sunt christiformia, necessario illa procedunt a christiformi.*

Baptism, one is adopted by God the Father as his child. Through Confirmation, one is empowered by God the Holy Ghost as his witness. Through Holy Orders, one is configured to the divine Son Jesus Christ as his priest. Being imprinted in our intellect, the three characters remain forever, even after death. As St Thomas Aquinas teaches, *Since, therefore, the subject of a character is the soul as to its intellective part, where faith resides, as stated above; it is clear that, the intellect being perpetual and incorruptible, a character cannot be blotted out from the soul.*[6] *Both grace and character are in the soul, but in different ways. For grace is in the soul, as a form having complete existence therein: whereas a character is in the soul, as an instrumental power.*[7]

The priestly character achieves a fuller configuration to Christ. As an instrumental power, the priestly character can be activated even though the priest may have lost God's grace. An apostate priest would validly offer Holy Mass and absolve dying penitents. This indicates a deeper configuration to Christ than is the case with holy Baptism and Confirmation. Those two sacraments indeed do not embed permanent divine powers[8] in the soul, since even a non-Christian can baptise in case of necessity, while a confirmed Christian cannot bear witness to Christ, through martyrdom for instance, if he has lost God's grace. But priests — and only priests — validly transubstantiate and absolve, even after they may have lost divine grace, tragically. Priests therefore bear the utmost sacramental configuration to Christ.[9] When ordained by the bishop, a successor of the Apostles appointed by Christ himself, the priest undergoes an ontological change. His soul is objectively modified

---

6 *Summa* III, 63, 5, c.

7 *Summa* III, 63, 5, ad 1.

8 We speak here of the power to convey or impart, not of that power to receive according to St Thomas Aquinas: 'the sacrament of Baptism pertains to recipients, since it confers on man the power to receive the other sacraments of the Church' cf. *Summa* III, 63, 6.

9 However, not the priesthood as such but charity is the ultimate configuration to God. This explains why for instance a laywoman like St Joan of Arc was surely closer to God while burning at the stake, than Bishop Cauchon who had condemned her to foster his political ambition.

by the sacramental character. The priestly character is more than a divine seal. It is a permanent capacity to posit divine actions as Christ's minister, regardless of the spiritual state of the priest.

In Persona Christi Capitis. For completion, the expression *in persona Christi* requires the word *capitis*, the Latin noun for 'head'. Acting 'in the person of Christ' thus requires a qualifier. What is meant here is not acting in the person of Christ as Judge, as Victim or as Priest, but as Head. Admittedly, these former aspects of Christ's role are included in the later, i.e. his capacity as Head. But the emphasis on Christ the Head points to his relationship to his members. Christ is the head of his mystical Body, the Catholic Church. Thus, acting *in persona Christi capitis* applies to those who facilitate the grafting of new members into the Body of the Church under the authority of Christ the Head; and who feed and strengthen these limbs once grafted. In a very broad sense this role may apply to any lay Catholics whose prayers, sacrifices and virtuous examples help increase the mystical Body of Christ. But in a strict sense, only priests act *in persona Christi capitis*, by virtue of the divine powers embedded in them at their ordination. Only priests can father souls to the life of grace as ministers of the sacraments: at holy Baptism,[10] through sacramental absolution and Extreme Unction. Only bishops can ordain other priests and administer Confirmation in their own right. Only priests can offer Holy Mass. Only priests[11] act as ordinary witnesses to the exchange of vows at Holy Matrimony; when receiving converts into the Church; and when preaching the doctrine of salvation. When so doing, priests act formally in the person of Christ the Head, fostering the growth of his mystical body the Church, until the number of the elect be fulfilled.

ANCIENT MASKS OFFER AN ETYMOLOGY FOR 'PERSON'

Long ago in Athens. The expression *in persona Christi capitis* focuses on the head of Christ rather than his entire body. Narrowing down further our investigation, we will now consider specifically

10 As its ordinary ministers by divine institution.
11 The new Code of Canon Law includes deacons by delegation.

the face of Christ, using the concept of a mask as an illustration. Thus, as indicated by St Thomas Aquinas,[12] an etymology for the word 'person' is *per-sonare*, literally: *sounding through*. In this sense, *persona* refers to the masks worn by actors in Greek and Roman amphitheatres, incorporating a small megaphone. Long before loud-speakers were invented, these devices were designed to amplify the voice so as to project the sound towards large audiences. Greek theatre had a religious purpose, originally, such as the worship of Dionysus at Athens; hence the ritual function of masks. Later on, theatrical performances portrayed ordinary life. The facial features, distinguishing the actors' masks, referred to identifiable social types such as the cook, the matron, the soldier, the maiden etc.

God enters the stage. In Christ, the human nature could be considered as the mask—the *persona* in this dramaturgical sense—used by the Word eternal to reach out to us. By nature, the divine Person of God the Son is invisible and dwells without space and time. Through the Incarnation, he united to himself a real human body and soul. Like an actor walking through the curtain, the divine Word, henceforth Jesus Christ, entered the stage of history where fallen men and women could see him and listen to him, thanks to his human body and soul. From the moment Our Lady answered 'Yes' to the Archangel Gabriel at the Annunciation, in her virginal womb a body and a soul started to exist, belonging immediately to the divine Person of God the Son.

Humanity is to Christ more than a mask. Christ's Body and Soul are to him, as Word eternal, like the mask to the actor in antiquity—a necessary device to manifest his identity to the human audience. It shows who he is and projects what he says. A crucial difference must be noted though. While an actor takes off his mask after the performance, the Word eternal will never repudiate the

12 'Boethius says (*De Duab. Nat.*): "The word person seems to be taken from those persons who represented men in comedies and tragedies. For person comes from sounding through [*personando*], since a greater volume of sound is produced through the cavity in the mask. These 'persons' or masks the Greeks called *prosopa*, as they were placed on the face and covered the features before the eyes.'" Cf. *Summa*, I, 29, art. 3, Obj 2.

true human body and soul he assumed once and for all. If ever a human actor literally 'became' his character—like a Hollywood film star being elected US President for instance—he would cease to be an actor. But the Word eternal became man for real, so that humanity is to him much more than a mask. It *is* him, even though it acts as an instrument. One could say that Christ's Body and Soul act *ut* persona *Verbi*—'as the persona of the Word.' Such is their dignity and their efficacy.

How this applies to priests . How does this apply to priests? When transubstantiating matter and absolving from sin, priests surrender body and soul to Christ, so that his divine power may act through them. This wilful suspension of the priest's person on behalf of Christ's divine Person puts the body and soul of the priest under the direct motion of Christ. When consecrating at Holy Mass and absolving in Confession, the priest becomes the *persona* of the Divine Saviour. The efficacy of these actions is beyond human capacity, but it operates through a human instrument,[13] both conscious and willing—the priest. In the noblest possible meaning of the word 'mask'—that is, a sacred tool designed to manifest the Godhead in action, priests can be considered the 'masks' of Christ, as Christ's humanity is the 'mask' of the Word eternal. As Hesychius of Jerusalem put it in his Commentary on the *Book of Leviticus* (written in the early fifth century), 'Priests do not extend the blessing by their own power, but because they bear the figure of Christ (*figuram ferunt Christi*), they are able, on account of him who is in them (*propter eum qui in ipsis est*), to extend the fullness of the blessing.'

Our Lady is the Word-carrier. The Blessed Virgin Mary who provided the Word Eternal with the human nature is a model for priests. As Dom Chautard wrote in *The Soul of the Apostolate* (#291), *[Mary] lives in Jesus, through Jesus, by His life, His love, and by union with His Sacrifice; and Jesus speaks in her and through her. Jesus is her life, and she is the Word-carrier, she amplifies His voice, she serves as His*

13   Cf. *Summa*, 3a, Q83, a1, 3um: 'the priest also bears Christ's image, in Whose person and by Whose power he pronounces the words of consecration.'

monstrance. This is manifested at the Visitation, when Our Lady's voice carries to St John the Baptist the presence of the Messiah; and also at Cana when she commands the servants, *Whatsoever he shall say to you, do ye* — *Quodcumque dixerit vobis, hoc facite* (Jn 2:5).

MARTYRDOM AS THE ULTIMATE IDENTIFICATION WITH CHRIST

Can we avoid martyrdom?. What would we do if faced with a choice between martyrdom and apostasy? It would be presumptuous to affirm that we would have the courage to profess Christ. In addition, considerations such as the fear of pain and our concern for those predictably affected by our demise may undermine our fidelity. Furthermore, prudence commands that we should explore every licit option to avoid death, instead of rashly exposing our lives. Is there no way to remain faithful to Christ in our hearts, then, while externally denying him? Priests faced with martyrdom are, so far, a minority. But if these considerations apply to Christians in general, they are of particular relevance to priests for two reasons. First, because priests have a higher responsibility to lead by example, after Christ the Good Shepherd who gave his life for his sheep. Second, because their status obliges priests daily to bear public witness of an invisible God, through visible signs, in a hostile world — which witness differs from martyrdom in degree only, not in kind. Let us frankly ask the following question then. As in Scorsese's film *Silence* referred to in a previous chapter, is there no way the words of the inquisitor could be true, when he urged Fr Rodrigues to trample upon the depiction of Christ, assuring him that, 'It's a formality, just a formality'?

Unity of the human person. To answer this crucial question, we need first to remember that the human person is one, the human soul being substantially united with the human body. Not even is the soul located in one particular part of the body, such as the brains or heart, leaving the rest of the body outside its reach. On the contrary, the human soul is coextensive to the body, which develops from conception inasmuch as shaped by the soul, and survives as long as animated by it. Their separation is death, which suspends personhood, so that a soul without its body is not truly a person anymore. It will become so again at the resurrection of the flesh, when God's omnipotence will restore that particular body to that particular soul. While on earth, nothing comes into our soul unless operating through our five physical senses. Reciprocally, everything our mind and will command our limbs to perform truly expresses our person. The more formal the visible gesture performed by our body, the more certain the adhesion of our soul to its invisible meaning. For instance, before a US President enters on the execution of his office, he takes a solemn Oath which binds him to govern in accordance with the Constitution. A more common example is when a betrothed man and woman exchange vows in church, they are then formally committed to love exclusive, fruitful and perpetual.

Rare and extreme circumstances may allow for cunning, as when underground priests use disguises and equivocation to escape unjust State officials. But when their identity is proven and when the State urges them to state or deny their faith, simulation is not permissible. This is why Our Lord, at first keeping silent before the Sanhedrin, finally made an answer: *The high priest asked him and said to him: Art thou the Christ, the Son of the Blessed God? And Jesus said to him: I am* (Mk 14:61-62). In such formal context, humans cannot escape the duty to use signs truthfully. Their gestures or words must express their convictions. Rather than moaning against this obligation as burdensome, just men rejoice in it because it demonstrates the beautiful unity of the human nature, body and soul, as designed by the Creator. It is because the material and spiritual components of our person are substantially one that we cannot claim a belief contrary to the signs we display. Particularly in a formal context, our external communication is deemed by men and by God to express our internal persuasion.

Unity of society. But God did not create each of us only as a unified entity. He designed us as social beings. We are fulfilled through life in society, after his own inner life as an uncreated society of Persons: Father, Son and Holy Ghost. Interaction among men being willed by God, impeding it offends him. Deceit harms social unity, while truthfulness fosters it. Consequently, a man or a woman urged by the State to confess or deny Christ and his Church owes it to God to answer sincerely. Failing to do so contradicts the unity of the person and of society, both willed by God. Thus, God cannot recognise as genuine a faith supposedly concealed in one's internal forum, while knowingly denied through unequivocal signs.

Unity of Christ. Truthfulness demonstrates the God-given unity of the human person and the God-willed unity of human society. Those goods are fully appreciated only in relation to Christ though. He is God made man: the invisible deity made perceptible to the senses of men. In Christ, the human nature is assumed by the divine nature irreversibly. In him human nature is united with the divine nature without confusion, but to a degree of unity which is unsurpassable. Faith in such a mystery is echoed by the unity of each human person. When at the cost of his earthly life, the martyr refuses to perform certain signs such as incensing an idol, he states the God-given unity of his human nature, which forbids dissimulation; and of society, harmed by deceit—while confessing the God-achieved unity of the Incarnation. The personal unity of the human body and soul echoes the personal unity of the human and divine natures in Christ.

Martyrdom is worship of Christ. This is why martyrdom is essentially an act of worship of Christ. The martyr states that he belongs to Christ individually and collectively. The martyr belongs to Christ individually because Christ is the type of humanity restored, to whom the Christian is conformed. The martyr belongs to Christ collectively, because Christ is the Head of his Mystical Body, the Church, of which every Christian is a member. The martyr accepts separation within his person through death inflicted, and from society through persecution undergone, with the deep conviction that Christ will restore unity, both to his person at the resurrection, and to society when gathering all the elect at the Last Judgement, while casting away the wicked. Martyrdom is cultic in its essence. It stresses the reality of the bond—in Christ—between the fallen material world and the invisible Rescuer. The martyr cannot make Christ appear in person in the midst of his persecutors, but through his sacrifice freely offered, he lets Christ demonstrate his power and manifest his presence.

Eucharistic martyrdom. This is supremely achieved when the context of martyrdom is Eucharistic as occurred for St Matthew the Evangelist,[14] St Thomas Becket,[15] St Stanislaus of Kraków ,[16] Bl. Noel Pinot[17] and recently the Servant of God Jacques Hamel.[18] Priests killed at the altar bear the most eminent witness to the reality of the divine presence, not only incarnate, but transubstantiated. When their blood is shed in the sanctuary, they act *in persona Christi* in the most literal and perfect way. The sacred Body and Blood of Christ their model lie upon the altar as separated under the Eucharistic species. Their blood soon lies similarly, mingled with his, upon the place of sacrifice. Nowhere is more eloquently professed the faith in the Saviour's loving power, who will raise his priests back to life on Judgement day, as he rose from the dead on Easter morning.

The blood of priests is known to God. In his woes to the Pharisees, Our Lord explicitly states that he will demand an account for the blood of his priests, *That upon you may come all the just blood that hath been shed upon the earth, from the blood of Abel the just, even unto the blood of Zacharias the son of Barachias, whom you killed between the temple and the altar* (Mt 23:35). Significantly, both men referred to by Our Lord were killed in connection with a ritual

14   Slain while offering Holy Mass, according to a pious tradition (depicted for example in Caravaggio's celebrated painting in the church of San Luigi dei Francesi in Rome).

15   The fearless Archbishop of Canterbury (1118–1170) chose to await his murderers in the sanctuary of his cathedral, the mother-church of England.

16   While offering Holy Mass, the patron saint of Poland and *Kraków* (1030–1079) was killed by the lustful king Boleslaw whom he had excommunicated.

17   This exemplary priest (1747–1794), pastor of Le Lourroux-Béconnais in Anjou, France, was arrested by the French Revolutionaries for being a Catholic priest. His judge was Citizen Roussel, an apostate priest who sentenced him to death. Hoping to increase the distress of his victim, Roussel had Fr Pinot's priestly vestments put on him. The place of execution in Angers was on the location of a church recently destroyed by the Revolutionaries. The guillotine was erected on the very spot where the altar used to stand. Aware of this, Fr Pinot walked up to it uttering the first words of Holy Mass, *Introibo ad altare Dei, ad Deum qui laetificat juventutem meam.* It was on a Friday afternoon at 3pm, the time of Our Lord's death on Calvary.

18   An old country priest killed by Islamists on 26 July 2016 in his rural church near Rouen, Normandy, France.

sacrifice, the main priestly function. They encompass the entire genealogy of the redemptive priesthood in the Old Testament, preparing the advent of the Sovereign High Priest, Our Lord. Abel, son of the first Adam, stands as its beginning, having been slain by Cain because God had accepted his sacrifice[19] and not his brother's. As for Zacharias, following Origen and St Basil, tradition identifies him with the father of Our Lord's Precursor, St Zachary, father of St John the Baptist. St Zacharias would have been killed by the Jews because he stood as a witness to the perpetual virginity of Our Blessed Lady and thus, indirectly, to the divine origin of the New Adam Our Saviour.

Priestly witness to the Blood of the Lord. While priests are not frequently slaughtered when offering Holy Mass though, they can all treat the hidden Saviour with as much reverence as if their lives were at stake. Unlike Uzzah whom God struck dead for daring to touch the ark of covenant,[20] priests on the contrary are given the mandate to handle the sacred species. While a culpable lack of Eucharistic reverence would normally not end the priest's earthly life, it would endanger his eternal life. St Paul's warning to the laity of Corinth applies even more to any priest: *For he that eateth and drinketh unworthily, eateth and drinketh judgement to himself, not discerning the body of the Lord* (1 Cor 11:29). The way a priest handles the Eucharistic species indicates his Eucharistic faith. Watching him respectfully, his parishioners will know by his gestures whether their priest believes and how far they might follow him: to the parish cafeteria, or further on toward the Cross and to a blessed eternity.

---

19 Reply to Objection 2. Adam, Isaac and other just men offered sacrifice to God in a manner befitting the times in which they lived, according to Gregory, who says (*Moral.* iv, 3) that in olden times original sin was remitted through the offering of sacrifices. Nor does Scripture mention all the sacrifices of the just, but only those that have something special connected with them. Perhaps the reason why we read of no sacrifice being offered by Adam may be that, as the origin of sin is ascribed to him, the origin of sanctification ought not to be represented as typified in him. Isaac was a type of Christ, being himself offered in sacrifice; and so there was no need that he should be represented as offering a sacrifice (cf. *Summa* 2-2, Q85, a2, Resp. to second objection).

20 Cf. 2 Sam 6:6–7.

MENTAL PRAYER AS UNION WITH CHRIST

No priest can fall gravely if he prays earnestly. No priest can fall gravely if he prays earnestly. Analysing the causes for the priestly crisis in modern times necessarily points to a problem with priestly prayer. Praying, so as to preach the Good News with fruit, was deemed a priority for the Apostles: *We will give ourselves continually to prayer and to the ministry of the word* (Acts 6:4). If a priest fails to pray, his fall is nigh. But what if a priest mistakes prayer with breathing techniques, and spiritual union with mental relaxation? We think that not a few priests (not to mention other consecrated persons and the laity) have been misled this way, with dire consequences for their spiritual life, their orthodoxy and their ministry.

The external similarities between Catholic contemplation and Zen meditation are well known. Since World War II, many Catholic contemplatives have attempted to draw from Oriental traditions.[21] Unlike liturgical prayer which requires codified phrasing and gestures, and unlike even meditation which ponders the givens of faith, contemplation leaves out any deliberate activity of the soul. The memory, intellect and will of the contemplative seek only to recall, know and desire nothing. But a lethal ambiguity lies here, demanding complete clarification. For Catholic contemplatives, nothingness — the *nada* of St John of the Cross — is not the goal, but a means to an end that is God Himself. Nothingness expresses the acknowledgement by the contemplative of his need to renounce every created activity in order to let himself be filled by the Uncreated God, a supremely personal entity. The Catholic contemplative is certain that God acts in him more powerfully when the evidence of the senses and intellectual assessment are sacrificed through a humble, prolonged and filial act of faith. Indeed, when after prayer the Catholic contemplative stands up again to fulfil the duties of his state, he knows that his understanding of what is to be done and his ability to fulfil it stem from the grace instilled in him by

---

21 Ancient Greece, was militarily vanquished by Rome, yet had conquered its victor culturally. Similarly, Zen Japan seems to have spiritually conquered its Christian American victor and its Western allies since World War II.

God during contemplation. On the contrary, the Oriental contemplative doesn't believe in personhood, either human or divine. Consequently, the nothingness he seeks leads to his annihilation as a rational subject and cannot connect him with a non-existing deity. This error stands in total opposition to Catholic contemplation. There, the believer knows himself to be someone, not something. He surrenders the use of his memory, intellect and will not to an impersonal whole, but to a well-identified personal God (i.e., his Creator, the Holy Trinity) and his Redeemer as God made Man, Jesus Christ. The peace experienced in this surrendering can be facilitated through learning and experience, but it remains fundamentally a gift from a loving God, received by the soul in grateful humility. In contradistinction, Oriental masters teach that techniques efficaciously raise the trained contemplative to spiritual fulfilment, of his own accord.[22]

No meta-dogmatic haven. Prayer being a chief duty and occupation of priests, many in the modern era were misled into false contemplation, forgetting the essential distinctions just stated. Their legitimate desire for universal peace and fraternity could be better fulfilled, they were told, by reaching and dwelling 'beyond dogmatic barriers.' They dived into Oriental 'contemplation' to escape dogmas, while often engaging in Marxism to end class conflict.[23]

---

22   Useful precisions on the delineation between prayer as an encounter with God and Eastern techniques can be found in the *Letter to the Bishops on some aspects of Christian meditation*, by Joseph Cardinal Ratzinger, Congregation for the Doctrine of the Faith, October 15, 1989.

23   In 1971, lapsed Christian John Lennon's song *Imagine* (co-written by his Japanese wife Yoko Ono) sounded like the new Gospel of that trend: 'Imagine there's no heaven / It's easy if you try / No hell below us / Above us only sky / Imagine all the people / Living for today... Aha-ah... / Imagine there's no countries / It isn't hard to do / Nothing to kill or die for / And no religion, too / Imagine all the people living life in peace... / You... / You may say I'm a dreamer / But I'm not the only one / I hope someday you'll join us / And the world will be as one / Imagine no possessions / I wonder if you can / No need for greed or hunger / A brotherhood of man / Imagine all the people / Sharing all the world... / You... / You may say I'm a dreamer / But I'm not the only one / I hope someday you'll join us / And the world will live as one.'

They forgot that human fulfilment is secured precisely through dogmas, which translate God's revelation for human souls, after Our Lord's petition to his Father: *Sanctify them in truth* (Jn 17:17). Even in our times, some Catholic priests and religious promote meditation in the Oriental fashion, seeking to provide a meta-dogmatic haven. Because such practices fall within private experience rather than being written statements expressly contradicting Catholic doctrine, they are deemed compatible with the Creed of the Church. Meanwhile, they actively undermine the faith of many:

1. in the personal nature of God and of the soul
2. in the absolute distinction between God as Creator and everything else as his creation
3. in the dignity of the body as substantially united to the soul
4. in the total gratuitousness of divine grace
5. in the necessity of conversion to Christ through his Church for salvation.

Referring back to the Japanese inquisitor's mantra in the film *Silence*, discussed in an earlier chapter: 'Japan is a swamp where Christianity cannot grow' — it seems that Zen bogged down many Western priests at the expense of their Catholic faith. This latent apostasy is extremely harmful to the souls of the shepherds, and of their flock. We therefore offer the following test to priests willing to assess whether their daily spiritual time is a prayer in the Catholic sense, or some relaxation after the Oriental fashion.

Between God and me, it must be personal. We suggest that the notion of personhood is the key. Whatever exists is either someone or something. It cannot be both. Prayer can only be from person(s) to Person(s), mainly from creatures to God (and secondarily among creatures when we on earth pray the saints and angels in heaven). Modern priests must ask themselves the question: By prayer, do I mean to communicate with *Someone*, or to dissolve into *something*? Between God and me, is it *personal*? Do I unite with God sought as a Person, or not?

Prayer can only be the former. The latter is not prayer at all. At best it is debatable relaxation—at worst it is demonic possession.[24] If prayer must be from person to Person, what is a person then? In particular, who are the invisible persons? We will now examine this topic.

RELATING TO INVISIBLE PERSONS

Most persons don't have a body. The classical definition of a person by Boethius (480–525 A.D.) is 'an individual substance of a rational nature.'[25] A person is a distinct entity endowed with reason and free will. Some persons have a body (i.e., humans) while other persons are pure spirits, either created (the angels, good or fallen) or uncreated (i.e., God the Father, God the Son and God the Holy Ghost). A Catholic priest prays when he seeks to enter in filial contact with the eminently personal triune God. The more personal his prayer, the more genuine it is. By personal we mean a communication between his created person as a believer and the three divine Persons within the Holy Trinity.[26] A priest engaged in genuine prayer daily—that is, with the only true God, Who is three *invisible* Persons—will learn to become ever more aware of other *invisible* persons, not only of visible ones.

St John teaches that our love for visible persons proves our love for invisible persons, namely the triune God: *He that loveth not his brother whom he seeth, how can he love God whom he seeth not?* (1 John 4:20). But if our love for the three divine—and non-visible—Persons is genuine, how can it not foster our love for other non-visible persons as well? The quality of our relationship with visible persons, especially those in need, expresses the genuineness of our love for God. Love or charity is the main theological virtue. But faith, another theological virtue, is better evidenced when priests show care for non-visible persons. The reason is that a

---

24 A homicidal 'someone' often lurks behind the unidentified 'something.'

25 *Naturæ rationalis individua substantia.*

26 In dependence on the Holy Trinity we can pray to holy created persons such as the Immaculate Mother of God, the saints and the holy angels.

priest's pastoral zeal is easily manifested through his immediate care of the people in the pews. But activism can produce similar effects. If doing a lot in a parish sufficed, Holy Mother Church would not have warned her priests against activism.[27] Pastoral zeal the more surely expresses theological charity as it encompasses non-visible persons, who can be reached only or mainly through theological faith, yielding no quantifiable reward. On the contrary, the same pastoral activity and achievements may express merely natural skills and aims if excluding non-visible persons. As any parish accountant will know, visible persons in the pews give tangible cash in the collection basket. But non-visible persons reward devout priests only with heavenly intercession and merits, currencies no bank will cash in and no supplier will accept. Therefore, the fact a priest will nevertheless spend time and energy interacting with such non-visible persons (without neglecting those he can see) is a sure sign of his faith and charity. Therefore, let us now consider the five categories of non-visible persons. The more a priest interacts with them, the more personal his relationship is with the three invisible divine Persons.

Created non-visible persons: five categories. First, a priest will believe in the holy angels and in fallen ones. He will publicly write and speak about them, seeking the protection of the former and begging for protection from the latter, not only for himself, but also for his parishioners. St Padre Pio of Pietrelcina is a good example of this.

Second, the priest will become familiar with the saints in heaven and their Queen, the Blessed Virgin Mary. He will interact with these invisible persons in his daily life, requesting their intercession on his behalf and for his parishioners; reading their lives in good hagiographies; preaching about them; extolling their virtues, celebrating their festivals with devotion and zeal, decorating their statues and images with flowers, and guiding parents in the selection of such saintly names for their children to be baptised.

---

27   The heresy of action was once termed 'Americanism,' after the Apostolic Letter *Testem Benevolentiae* which Pope Leo XIII addressed to Cardinal Gibbons on 22 January, 1899.

Third, the priest will become more sensitive to persons not only invisible, but also vulnerable, unlike the angels and saints. This applies first to the adorable Person[28] of the Lord Jesus hidden under the Eucharistic species. In the sacred chalice and ciborium, the God-made-Man entrusts His true Body, Blood, Soul and Divinity to his priest. He lets his priest handle him. Caring with awe for the Eucharistic Lord according to the rubrics and prescriptions of the Church, is a further sign that the priest's private prayer is genuine, i.e. truly addressed to the personal God.

Other invisible and helpless persons[29] need the priest's attention. They are the holy souls in Purgatory. Those fellow-believers died in the state of grace, but some unexpiated sins delay their entrance into Paradise. They cannot help themselves. But the living can offer sacrifices for the accelerated purification of those souls, obtaining for them a quicker entrance into heaven where they will start enjoying the beatific vision. A priest who reminds the congregation of the need to pray for a deceased person at a funeral Mass demonstrates genuine care for this invisible person. For the same reason, he will also offer votive Requiem Masses for the holy souls in general, especially during the month of November dedicated to them. He will explain the beautiful dogma of Purgatory and the consoling doctrine of intercession. He will also teach his flock about the importance and efficacy of the indulgences, whereby the living can obtain from God's mercy immediate entrance of a holy soul into paradise. Above all, that priest will stress the unsurpassable power of the offering of the Holy Sacrifice of the

28   The Person of Christ is the Word Eternal considered in his substantial and irrevocable assumption of the human nature. The Person of Our Lord is not created but divine. We mention it here only because it is forever united to his human nature whose created elements indicate his presence to us, albeit under the veil of Eucharistic species.

29   Strictly speaking, the personhood of the Holy Souls (as of any dead human being) is suspended by death until the reunion with their bodies at the Last Judgement. Here we refer to them as persons because their personhood will ultimately be reactivated to enjoy everlasting bliss, which the prayers of the living help them to enter once purified, even before their bodies are restored to them.

Mass for the prompter purification of the holy souls through the infinite merits of the Passion and Death of the Saviour.

After the angels and saints, after the Eucharistic Lord and the holy souls, a priest who prays daily to the personal and invisible triune God will relate to further invisible persons, supremely helpless and vulnerable. Those are the unborn. To refer back to the title of Scorsese's film, a deafening *silence* characterises the pastoral incapacitation of an entire generation of bishops and priests as regards the safeguarding of unborn children. Since the 1960s, the silence about abortion thundered from church pulpits and in parish newsletters. Over half a century after *Humanae Vitae*,[30] when the connection between contraception and abortion has been amply demonstrated, and while new technologies threaten antenatal life more perniciously than ever, such as IVF from two or more parents, surrogacy, embryonic screening and harvesting—the incapacity of most clerics to preach the Gospel of Life[31] is a troubling symptom. While abortion affects society as one among many other social and economic problems, yet this evil harms humanity at such a core level that no effort for peace can succeed unless the tragedy of abortion is acknowledged and remedied. On the scale of harm to humanity, other threats are to abortion what acne is to bowel cancer on the scale of bodily ailments: not pleasant, but survivable. Ignoring the precedence of abortion or playing down its impact is a widespread error even among well-meaning clerics.[32]

Five symptoms of a loss of contact with invisible persons. The faith of a priest in a personal God reaching him in contemplation

30 Issued by Pope Paul VI on 29 July 1968.

31 Pope John Paul II released his master encyclical *Evangelium Vitae* (i.e. *The Gospel of Life*) on the feast of the Annunciation, 25th March 1995.

32 'It seems a little strange that we [Catholics] are so wildly exercised about the "murder" (and the word is of course correct) of an unborn infant by abortion, or even the prevention of conception which is hardly murder, and yet accept without a qualm the extermination of millions of helpless and innocent adults, some of whom may be Christians and even our friends rather than our enemies. I submit that we ought to fulfil the one without omitting the other.' Cf. Thomas Merton, *Cold War Letters*, (Maryknoll: Orbis Books, 2007), 38. (Letter to Dorothy Day, Dec. 20, 1961).

and in Holy Communion must spontaneously and increasingly awake in him faith in and love for angelic and human persons including invisible and vulnerable ones, whether dead or unborn. On the contrary, the five following symptoms betray a loss of contact with invisible persons:

1. scorning devotion to the holy angels and presenting evil as a mere phenomenon instead of connected with fallen angels, i.e. persons
2. never or seldom mentioning Our Lady and the saints in public and omitting to refer to them in private
3. a casual handling of the Eucharistic species
4. canonisation speeches delivered instead of intercession at funeral homilies
5. a constant silence from the pulpit and in the confessional about abortion and contraception.

In the life of such a priest, created invisible persons play no role: namely, the persons of the holy angels and saints; of the Eucharistic Lord Jesus;[33] those of the holy souls in Purgatory and of children in the womb. Such a loss of contact will lead to a loss of faith in the very existence of these persons. As symptoms, these grave deficiencies in the ministry of a priest cast a very serious doubt about his prayer life. Does he pray? As explained earlier, we are not considering here the case of priests who devote no or insufficient time to formal prayer. Their problem is much easier to identify and to solve. Rather, our concern here is about the priest who thinks he prays, perhaps over an hour daily, when in reality he does not. He is victim of the lethal confusion described earlier between genuine prayer (i.e., a relationship from person to Person) and Oriental fakes (i.e., a suicidal denial of personhood). While such an error

---

33 As pointed in a previous footnote, the Person of Our Lord is not created but divine. We mention it here only because it is forever united to his human nature whose created elements indicate his presence to us, albeit under the veil of Eucharistic species.

is not by itself culpable, if the priest was simply misled by false masters and bad books, it is nevertheless harmful to his faith and flock. Furthermore, since true prayer is the breathing of the soul, false contemplation is a threat to our salvation: the lungs of our soul must inhale the Divine Breath, i.e. the personal God, while our heart still beats. As Genesis teaches: *the Lord God . . . breathed into [the man's] face the breath of life* (2:7). And in the New Testament, the New Adam Our Lord *breathed on [the apostles]; and he said to them: "Receive ye the Holy Ghost"* (Jn 20:22).

THE BLESSED VIRGIN MARY CONFIGURES PRIESTS TO HER SON JESUS

The human race was stripped of divine grace by the devil when Adam and Eve committed the original sin. God had to provide garments for their bodies as a remedy. Later on the Eternal Word 'put on' our human nature at his Incarnation as the New Adam, so that our souls may gradually 'put on Christ.' This applies to any baptised person, but more intensely to those called to a sacramental configuration to Christ in Holy Orders: seminarians, priests and bishops. The New Eve, Our Blessed Lady, is actively involved in that process.

The Lord Jesus was formed in the virginal womb of his Immaculate Mother, the Blessed Virgin Mary. She gave him his human nature, she formed him as a child and a young man and accompanied him at every stage in his mission. She can configure us to Jesus effortlessly too, as through a process of organic growth, as St Louis de Montfort assures us. Our Lady offers such assistance to all men, but particularly to priests, whose souls share in her Son's divine powers. Just as she stood at the foot of the Cross as co-redemptrix, the Blessed Virgin Mary stands by us attentively at Holy Mass, the unbloody re-presentation of the Sacrifice of Calvary.

The vesting of the priest in the sacristy . The vesting of the priest in the sacristy before Holy Mass can be compared with the very process of gestation of Christ the High Priest in Our Lady's bosom. Once fully vested, the celebrant exits the sacristy, as after nine months Our Lord left his Mother's virginal womb at Christmas. In both cases the priest directs his steps towards the place of sacrifice — the altar in the sanctuary standing for the Cross on Calvary — the purpose of his journey. Let us now consider this analogy,[34] whereby the visible vesting symbolises the spiritual configuring of the priest to Christ his model so as to offer the salutary Sacrifice *in persona Christi*. Seven ritual prayers[35] express those various stages.

34 It is eloquently developed by St Vincent Ferrer O.P. in his *Life of Our Lord*:

'The first thing done for our sake by Our Lord and Saviour Jesus Christ was His most noble and most wonderful Incarnation, when He came down from heaven and enthroned Himself in the bosom of Mary Ever Virgin, and clothed Himself therein with our vesture, that is, with our human nature; for His Godhead was hidden beneath the veils of His human nature.

'This wonderful work is symbolised in the Mass when the priest enters the sacristy, thereby representing the entrance of the Son of God within the virginal bosom of His Virgin Mother, wherein He was clothed with our nature.

'The devout Christian may contemplate three things here: First, as relics, vestments, and other church ornaments are kept in the sacristy, so also in the glorious shrine of the virginal bosom there were relics — the power of God the Father, the wisdom and person of God the Son, and the operative grace of God the Holy Ghost. Vestments, too, were there — to wit, Grace and Virtue, since the fullness of Grace and of Virtue was found in Mary Ever Virgin; while the ornaments with which our great High Priest was to offer sacrifice on the Altar of the Cross on Good Friday were present in the most noble and most sacred Body of Jesus Christ, which was formed from the pure and immaculate blood of His Mother.

'Secondly; the laity do not see the priest vesting in the sacristy, though they believe he is vesting, and hope he will come forth soon. When the Great High Priest, Jesus Christ, was vested in the virginal womb of Mary, the Jewish people knew it not, nor did they behold the mystery, for His Incarnation was hidden and silent. But the faithful ones believed that He would come, that He would become Man, and would be born of a Virgin, as had been foretold by many of the prophets.

'Thirdly, the priest puts on seven different vestments — the soutane, if he be but a simple priest; the rochet, if he be a bishop; the cowl, if he be a monk; then the amice, alb, girdle, maniple, stole, and chasuble. So also in the bosom of Mary Our High Priest vested Himself with the seven gifts of the Holy Ghost, wherewith the Most Holy Body of Our Lord was endowed and adorned (cf. Is xi., 2–3). This is the first work which is represented by the Holy Sacrifice.'

35 Their use is recommended for celebrants of the Ordinary form of the Roman rite as explained by the Holy See's Office for the Liturgical Celebrations of the Supreme Pontiff (cf. http://www.vatican.va/news_services/liturgy/details/ns_lit_doc_20100216_vestizione_en.html, last accessed 16 March 2020).

First, when washing his hands, the priest says: *Give manly power to my hands, O Lord, in order to cleanse every stain, so that I may be able to serve you without defilement of mind and body.* This demonstrates the intention of God when becoming man, that is, to act with strength in order to restore to sanctity our fallen nature stained by sin.

Second, the priest then spreads upon his head and neck the amice: a rectangular piece of white cloth symbolizing the helmet of salvation and a sign of resistance against temptation. He says: *Place, O Lord, on my head the helmet of salvation, that I may overcome the assaults of the devil.* Just like Our Lord came not as an idle man but as an idol fighter, to destroy every false god fabricated by Satan.

Third, the priest dons the alb, a white linen tunic which covers his whole body, signifying integrity. He says: *Purify me, O Lord, from all stain and cleanse my heart, that, washed in the blood of the Lamb, I may enjoy eternal delights.* This refers again to the intimate identification with Christ granted only through the shedding of his precious Blood, that is, through sacrificial configuration with the Lamb of God.

Fourth, the priest then ties the cincture, a cord which fastens the alb to the waist and stands for purity: *Gird me, O Lord, with the cincture of purity, and quench in my heart the fire of concupiscence, that the virtue of continence and chastity may remain in me.* Like Christ his model, the priest has freely renounced all exclusive love for creatures, so as to convey to all of them the Good News of salvation.

Fifth, the maniple is the band of cloth hanging on the priest's left forearm. It was originally a towel with which the Roman orators wiped the sweat off their foreheads. When saying the prayer: *Let me deserve, O Lord, to bear the maniple of tears and sorrow, so that one day I may come with joy into the rewards of my labours*, the priest is reminded of the fact that like Christ, he is coming to toil and suffer, as a condition for victory.

Sixth, the stole is the long band that fits around the neck, a symbol of immortality and the sign of the dignity of the priesthood. While taking the stole the priest says: *Restore to me, O Lord, the robe of immortality which was lost to me by my first parents, and, although I am unworthy to approach your sacred mysteries, grant me nevertheless eternal joy.* This prayer states explicitly the purpose of the Incarnation, that is, to restore our fallen human nature and bring the whole human race into an even higher felicity in the presence of God.

Seventh and last, the chasuble is the outermost vestment worn by the celebrant at Mass, and the emblem of charity, which makes the yoke of Christ light and agreeable. The priest then says: *O Lord, who said, "My yoke is sweet and my burden light," grant that I may carry it so as to obtain your grace. Amen.* This prayer insists on the identification with Christ in whom there is fortitude but no harshness; no weakness but meekness.

A seven-year walk toward the altar of God. Just as Christ left his mother's virginal womb and entered into the world for one purpose, namely, to glorify his Father through the redemptive Sacrifice of the Cross, the priest, now vested, walks through the door of the sacristy and enters the sanctuary, towards the altar of God where he will re-present Christ's unique Sacrifice.

Christ came sacrificially to manifest God's presence and love among his people, and priests live among people to manifest Christ's presence and love for them all. Just as the priest vesting in the sacristy imitates Christ's Incarnation whose only aim was our Redemption, the faithful are to learn about Christ through the saintly behaviour of their pastors, which they must imitate. Hence did St Paul exhort the faithful 'to put on Christ,' organising their entire lives as a sacred vesting with grace, in view of judgement and eternity.

This configuration of the priest to Christ didn't happen overnight though. The seven-year formation at seminary could be considered as an antechamber to the priesthood—as the seven-minute-or-so vesting in the sacristy is to the offering of Holy Mass. Year by year, the seminarian is gradually configured to Christ the Sovereign High Priest. One could transpose what was just explained about the ritual vesting in the sacristy before Holy Mass, counting one whole year at seminary for every minute in the sacristy.

Priestly formation traditionally begins with the *Tonsure*, when the candidate renounces worldly allurements. The bishop cuts off five pieces of hair on the four sides and on the top of his head, a symbolic marking of the future priest with the Five Wounds of Christ, received at his crucifixion in his four limbs and side. The young man becomes liturgically a cleric[36] and is clothed with the black cassock and white surplice.

Then comes the first minor ordination, when the seminarian is made a *Porter*, entrusted with the care of the sacred building and with the duty to expel those who may cause trouble in the holy place. He is to stand up for the rights of the Most High and to be ready to suffer for the honour of the House of God.

He is later ordained a *Lector* or 'Reader,' mandated to proclaim the Lessons of the very Word of God and to bless the bread and new fruits, already participating in Christ's mission of sanctifying Creation.

The third, less remote, participation in the priesthood of Christ is the seminarian's ordination as an *Exorcist*. Our Lord came to put an end to the devil's tyranny over Creation, and in particular over men through sin. The future priest is thus already associated with that mission.

The fourth minor order of *Acolyte* includes lighting the candles on the altar, carrying them in procession and during the solemn singing of the Gospel; preparing wine and water for the Holy Sacrifice of the Mass, and assisting the sacred ministers at Holy Mass.

The first major order is the *Subdiaconate*.[37] Following this, one may pour wine into the chalice at the altar, read the Epistles before

---

36   Under the 1983 Code of Canon Law, the clerical state is entered through diaconal ordination. Without prejudice for canonical discipline, the Church's intention as expressed in the rite of Tonsure, licitly conferred, is to consecrate the candidates to God's liturgical service.

37   'Historically, the earliest mention of the subdiaconate seems to be found in the letter of Pope Cornelius (A.D. 255) to Fabius of Antioch, in which he states that, there are among the Roman clergy forty-six priests, seven deacons, and seven subdeacons. There is nothing to indicate, however, that the subdiaconate is not older than the third century. That there were subdeacons in the African Church in the same century is evident from the letters of St. Cyprian (e.g. Epistle 8)' (cf. http://www.newadvent.org/cathen/14320a.htm, accessed 16 March 2020).

the people and carry out the ritual washing of the sacred linens used for the Holy Sacrifice. The *Subdeacon* is thus admitted to a more intimate union with Christ through the care for the sacrificial gifts and linens so essentially connected with the offering of the divine Victim.

The *Deacon* may proclaim the Holy Gospel and can preach. He may handle the sacred vessels and even assist the priest in administering the sacraments. Thus, the diaconate is like the last vestment put on by the candidate during his formative configuration to Christ at seminary.

Finally, the seminarian is ordained a *Priest*, his seventh ordination or the seventh degree of his sacramental configuration to Christ. Eventually he stands at the altar of God, fully vested with each of his seven priestly vestments[38] as an embodiment of his seven ordinations, that progressive participation in Christ's very priesthood, with which his human nature was clothed during his seminary formation. The priestly character has now[39] been imprinted in his soul, there for ever to remain, either to his dire shame in hell, or to his glory in heaven.

If ever ordained a bishop, that priest would receive the fullness of Christ's priesthood. In addition to the other sacraments, he would be able to ordain other priests and confer the Sacrament of Confirmation in his own right. This sacramental configuring to the Sovereign High Priest would be displayed at Holy Mass vestimentarily, as the pontiff would process to the altar of sacrifice bearing the Five Wounds of Christ the Victim: on his gloves and slippers would shine four embroidered crosses, while upon his chest would hang his pectoral cross.[40] The bishop will not have forgotten his

38   It is seven if the priest wears the biretta in addition to his chasuble, stole, maniple, cincture, alb and amice.

39   Technically, the sacramental character of Holy Orders is imprinted in the cleric's soul even before priestly ordination, as stated by the *Catechism of the Catholic Church* #1570: 'The sacrament of Holy Orders marks [deacons] with an *imprint* ("character") which cannot be removed and which configures them to Christ, who made himself the "deacon" or servant of all.'

40   Normally visible to all if the pontiff wears a cope; or if he wears a chasuble, then enlarged in the cross-shaped patterns adorning the front and back of that other vestment.

own Tonsure ceremony, when the cutting of five locks of his hair anticipated his sacramental configuration to Christ, now accomplished. One may admire the harmony and sense of purpose of Holy Mother Church when training her sons as future priests: at the very first step, the Tonsure, the young man is marked with the Five Wounds which will, so to speak, grow in size and glow when displayed upon his vestments if he becomes a bishop. Whether priest or bishop, the minister acts *in persona Christi* supremely when serving at the altar also marked with five crosses at each corner and in the middle, for it also symbolises Christ.

Our Lady stands by her priest when he offers Holy Mass, as she stood by her divine Son at Calvary. As it happens, the prayer said by the pontiff when putting on his gloves indirectly reminds us of the fact that Our Lady attends the vesting of her Son's priest. That prayer indeed recalls the loving stratagem whereby, in the Book of Genesis, Jacob's mother covered his hands with the skin of the goat so as to secure his father's blessing: *Place upon my hands, Lord, the cleanliness of the new man, that came down from heaven; that, just as Jacob Thy beloved, covering his hands with the skins of goats, and offering to his father most pleasing food and drink, obtained his father's blessing, so also may the saving victim offered by our hands, merit the blessing of Thy grace. Through our Lord Jesus Christ, Thy Son, Who in the likeness of sinful flesh offered Himself for us.*[41]

Our Lady clothes us with her Son's virtues. To summarise the detailed explanation of the vesting given earlier, let us remember that Our Lady stands in the sacristy behind us as we vest before Holy Mass. She sets upon our head and spreads on our shoulders the helmet of salvation, the amice. She clothes us with the wedding garment, the alb immaculate. She ties around our waist the cincture of purity. She sets on our wrist the maniple to sow in sorrow and harvest in joy. She smoothes against our chest the stole of immortality and unfolds over us the sweet and light yoke of her Son, the chasuble. She walks with us to the altar of God, 'of God who gives joy to our youth,' and she intercedes with us as we offer

41   Cf. Gn 27:6–29 and Rom 8:3.

to the glory of the Father the divine Victim, their Son, our Lord, for the salvation of the world; as we offer our own poor priestly selves as well in him; as we offer the sorrows, contrition, joys and hopes of our little congregation and of the Church universal.

Because we priests remain such even outside of Holy Mass, Our Lady still stands by us to clothe us with the virtues of her Son Jesus, long before we vest in the sacristy, and well after we unvest. The prayers traditionally said by clerics first thing in the morning when putting on their clothes bear witness to this. They refer to the evangelical counsels of poverty, chastity and obedience. Not only religious but secular clerics as well used to recite these prayers when dressing.

For the cassock: *O Lord, the portion of my inheritance and my chalice, You are He who will restore my inheritance to me. Amen.*[42] This prayer expresses the cleric's death to worldly possessions, for the sake of gaining Christ and being granted access to the Father's eternal kingdom. Indeed, the black cassock can be seen as a shroud separating the man of God from earthly goods. This prayer is the one spoken by the bishop when tonsuring the cleric. The cutting of the five pieces of hair symbolises this willing loss of created adornments so as to put on Christ.

When putting on the collar (still in his bedroom) the cleric prays: *Set me under your sweet yoke, O Lord, and that of Mary your Mother.*[43] This prayer petitions for the grace of the virtue of obedience. The submission of the will is joyful and fruitful when meant to conform to the will of the Sovereign High Priest Jesus Christ and of his Immaculate Mother. This surrender will bear the fruit of humility and meekness, after our priestly Model who taught: *Take up my yoke upon you, and learn of me, because I am meek and humble heart.... For my yoke is sweet and my burden light.*[44]

Finally, when tying the cincture around his waist, the cleric requests: *Gird me, O Lord, with the cincture of purity, and quench*

---

42 *Dominus, pars hereditatis meae et calicis mei, tu es qui restitues hereditatem meam mihi. Amen.*
43 *Subjice me, Domine, dulci jugo tuo dulcique jugo Matris tuae Mariae.*
44 Mt 11:29–30.

in my heart the fire of concupiscence, that the virtue of continence and chastity may abide in me.[45] He will pray the same prayer when vesting for Holy Mass in the sacristy if he is in major orders. We can admire the wisdom of Holy Mother Church, no doubt speaking for Our Lady herself, who knows well how necessary the virtue of chastity is for those who are to imitate the virginal Saviour. The current crisis of sexual abuse committed by clergy demonstrates that begging God daily for this specific virtue is no luxury. Clerics failing to wear clericals deny themselves this protection. While those wearing only a clergyman suit may avail themselves of the prayer for the collar, requesting the fundamental virtue of obedience, they still leave out the two prayers for the cassock and cincture, specifically asking for poverty and chastity.

Lastly, for liturgical functions even outside of Holy Mass, such as the choral recitation of the Divine Office, or the blessing of holy objects, or the administering of most other sacraments and sacred functions, the cleric would don over his cassock the white surplice saying: *Invest me, O Lord, as a new man, who was created by God in justice and the holiness of truth. Amen.*[46] Again, this prayer was pronounced by the bishop during the Tonsure ceremony, when he clothed the new cleric with the immaculate livery of Christ, the Sovereign High Priest.

CONCLUSION

This chapter sought to unfold the riches encompassed in the well-known expression *in persona Christi*. We priests act *in persona Christi capitis*, that is, 'in the person of Christ the Head' especially when offering the Holy Sacrifice of the Mass. But just as each Holy Mass must inspire our entire day, we must learn to act in the Person of Christ in everything we do. We examined this expression from the successive angles of Christology, of the Holy Trinity, of the sacraments, of etymology, of martyrdom and of the liturgy.

---

45   *Praecinge me, Domine, cingulo puritatis, et exstingue in lumbis meis humorem libidinis; ut maneat in me virtus continentiae et castitatis.*

46   *Indue me, Domine, novum hominem, qui secundum Deum creatus est in iustitia et sanctitate veritatis. Amen.*

In part One, reflecting on what the person of Christ is, we observed that the three divine Persons of God the Father, God the Son and God the Holy Ghost are fulfilled, not hindered, through mutual interaction in the unity of the Most Holy Trinity. We deduced that so it must be also for human persons, as exemplified by Christ's humanity, brought to unsurpassed perfection through its union with the Person of God the Son. The sacramental characters imprinted in our soul at holy Baptism and Confirmation configure us humans to Christ. This is supremely the case for the priestly character.

In part Two, we observed that the ancient masks of Greek actors provide an etymological illustration of the concept of person. We applied this analogically to the Incarnation, whereby Christ's human nature can be seen as the 'persona' of the Word Eternal. In the noblest sense of the term 'mask' or *persona*, priests can be seen as 'personas' of Christ.

In part Three we concluded that martyrdom is the ultimate identification with Christ. Martyrs bear witness to the unity of the human person, of society and of Christ respectively. This is supremely the case for priests martyred in connection with the Holy Eucharist, as their flesh and blood lie sacrificed by the church altar, mingled with those of the sacrificed Lord, their Model.

Part Four led us to examine mental prayer as union with Christ. We were reassured that no priest could fall gravely if he prayed, as Catholic contemplation strengthens the priest. But we were warned against Eastern techniques (as distinct from genuine prayer), which ignore personhood, thus threatening prayer life and undermining our union with Christ.

In part Five, we extended the interpersonal nature of the Catholic contemplation of God to our interaction with non-visible created persons. A genuine relationship with the three divine Persons and with Christ in particular must lead to relating to other non-visible persons. These persons fall into five categories: the holy angels (and the fallen ones); Our Lady and the saints; the Eucharistic Lord; the Holy Souls in Purgatory; unborn children.

Lastly, part Six focused on the Blessed Virgin Mary's ability to configure us priests to her Son Jesus. We remarked that the seven vesting prayers in the sacristy before Holy Mass are like a liturgical Incarnation. This summarizes the process of priestly formation during which seven orders are imparted to the seminarian over seven years. This vestimentary and sacramental configuration of the priest to Christ through Our Lady is strengthened every morning when the cleric commits afresh to obedience, poverty and chastity while putting on his collar, cassock and cincture.

The great paradox is that our personality is respected and fulfilled inasmuch as we invite Christ to take possession of us. This applies to all men, since all were created in Christ as the Eternal Word, and all were redeemed in Christ as the New Adam and Saviour. Through priestly ordination though, God's unfathomable wisdom brings such configuration to its ontological culmination. We priests have the glorious task of collaborating with such a grace through our sacramental and pastoral ministry to souls, increasing the mystical Body of Christ the Head. We know that this requires our ever more faithful imitation of Christ the Good Shepherd, our Model. May he and his Immaculate Mother have mercy on our weakness and radiate their love and sanctity through our daily actions.

5

Unfolding the Holy Shroud

BISHOPS ARE TEACHERS OF THE PEOPLE BY divine mandate, and we priests assist them in this glorious ministry. In our homilies at Holy Mass, through spiritual guidance in and out of the confessional, in catechism classes, through articles, online posts and conferences, we strive to share with every soul the Good News of the Redemption according to their needs and circumstances. While we may sometimes wish to innovate as to formulations and illustrations, we know we are called to convey truths already revealed and perennial, that is, unchangeable. At no level of the Church Hierarchy is novelty ever to be expressed if this innovation is understood as undermining or contradicting the deposit of the Catholic faith. And yet, as expert theologians as well as parish homilists experience, this doctrinal fidelity does not frustrate our creativity, nor does it mean inflicting monotony on our congregation. How permanence in faith fosters freshness in expression is a mystery we should like to explore in this chapter.

All throughout Church history, new doctrinal statements have been issued as part of the Magisterium, in fulfilment of the Church's teaching mission. In what sense are they new? Such pronouncements can never contradict earlier ones. They can only make more explicit what has always been part of Divine Revelation, consisting of Scripture and Tradition. The Hierarchy of the Church and her theologians gradually unfold revealed truth, in accordance with the parable of Our Lord: *Every scribe instructed in the kingdom of heaven, is like to a man that is a householder, who bringeth forth out of his treasure new things and old* (Mt 13:52). The data of the faith is not to be invented or imported, even less constructed, but merely expounded under the guidance of the Holy Ghost: *The Paraclete,*

the Holy Ghost, whom the Father will send in my name, He will
teach you all things, and bring all things to your mind, whatsoever
I shall have said to you (Jn 14:26).

To explain the development of Catholic doctrine, we offer an
analogy between unfolding Christ's Holy Shroud and developing
Christ's Revelation. The purpose in each case is to display the full
figure of Christ, either visually on the cloth, or doctrinally through
magisterial promulgations. On Easter morning then, St Peter, St
John and St Mary Magdalene found the empty linens wrapped
together in the empty tomb. Some time on that day, they would
have taken with them the precious relics. Back in the Upper Room,
with what emotion they would have slowly unfolded the shroud,
gradually displaying the Master's silhouette: first his shoulder, then
his elbow, now his foot and then his Head.... Everywhere, their
eyes would meet so many wounds, all endured for their redemption—and for ours.[1]

Upon Christ's folded Shroud as within Christ's revelation, the
entirety of the message is present from the start—albeit hidden.
Consequently, the Church cannot add anything new to the data
given. She can only unfold Christ's silhouette and make explicit
his Good News. She bears witness to growth, like a mother to the
child in her womb, or like astronomer Father Georges Lemaître
theorising universal expansion (later known as the Big Bang the-
ory). In each case, a core truth is given and development follows.
How long will the unfolding of Christ's Revelation take? It will
take until Christ returns. The completion of this work of patience,
love and humility will mark the end of time. Then Christ will
appear before all eyes, radiating his Good News as a reward of
glory for the just, and as retribution for those who will have shut
their minds to his truth and their hearts to his mercy.

---

1   Please note that it is irrelevant to our analogy whether or not the Turin
Shroud is indeed the one in which the Saviour lay buried. What is certain is
that there was such a shroud, and that none more scientifically convincing
than the Turin one has surfaced.

CONSIDERING THE HOLY SHROUD

What does the Holy Shroud look like? It is a depiction of Our Lord's tortured Body (both back and front), spread across the 14.5-feet-long by 1.4-foot-wide linen cloth, with such accuracy that this sacred relic has been termed 'The Fifth Gospel.' The Holy Shroud—presently kept in Turin, Italy—is the most tested object in the world. The scientific findings, due to their number and complexity, now constitute a distinct branch of science called sindonology, after the word *sindon*, the Greek word for 'shroud.'

Let us recall a few sindonological discoveries. It took nineteen centuries to realise that the Shroud is a photographic negative: inversing paler and darker areas reveals the actual picture. Further analysis established that the depiction results from irradiation, not from the application of pigments upon the linen material. Later on, the image was found to be three-dimensional, allowing the shaping of a resin model of Our Lord's Body as when it was lying wrapped in the Shroud. Anomalies such as the absence of an image of the thumb on either hand were explained, while microscopic examination found diverse pollens from the Middle East stuck in the fibres of the cloth.

Thus, the Holy Shroud of Christ yields its secrets by stages, and yet, all the information has been present on the material since Easter morning. Similarly, Christian doctrine develops across time, even though Christ's Revelation was completed when Christ's last apostle died. For example, in 451 the Council of Chalcedon defined that Christ had two natures, one human and one divine, united under one single divine self. But these truths had been contained in Christ's Revelation from the start. Another example: in 1215 the Council of Lateran defined the Eucharistic change as *Transubstantiation*, not inventing a new belief, but explaining an original truth. Hence, just as no genuine scientist would add to the Holy Shroud data from without, equally, no Catholic theologian can ever increase Christ's Revelation. Scientists will apply to the Holy Shroud modern technology and the resources of their intellect to find further evidence. Similarly, Catholic theologians rely on their skills and inspiration to draw new conclusions from pre-existing truths. In either case, new investigations can only build upon earlier findings.

The following episode in the Shroud examinations illustrates this principle *a contrario*. In 1989, Carbon 14 tests seemed to establish that the Holy Shroud dated from the Middle Ages. But leading researcher Raymond Rogers changed his mind on discovering that the samples tested were not part of the original material. They belonged instead to the repairs undergone by the Shroud after the 1532 fire in Chambery. It appeared that medieval cotton threads had been expertly woven into the original linen fabric to mend fire damage. This applies analogically to the work of theologians probing Christ's Revelation. Any theological statement one may proffer in contradiction with Christ's Revelation rests upon unauthentic premises (and fosters a non-Catholic agenda). Like the Carbon 14 findings, such unorthodox statements may sound convincing when issued, but like them, they are flawed at some level, hence unscientific. '

WHY HOLY CHURCH TAKES HER TIME

Holy Mother Church tells us all truth about God. She does not tell it all at once though — for three reasons. First, God is infinite, whereas our human intelligence is limited of its nature, and obscured by sin, so that we need time to explore the truth. Second, unlike angels who understand by intuition or immediate grasp, we humans reach the truth gradually, inferring causes from consequences. Third, the Church reacts to historical circumstances: whether adverse ones such as heresies and wars, or favourable ones such as the deeds of saints or even the discoveries of scientists. By God's Providence, the Church's response to circumstances leads her to focus on this or that specific aspect of the revealed truth, while further aspects will only be examined later on. For instance, the Church's pro-life teaching was intensely developed in the past fifty years in response to institutionalised abortion.

These three factors help us understand the development of doctrine. Development here expresses inner growth and precludes addition from without. This is the capital point to understand:

whenever the Church makes a new pronouncement, it is never new in relation to God's Revelation, but only in relation to contemporary believers. For example, when the Divine Motherhood of Our Lady was defined at the Council of Ephesus in 431, it was new inasmuch as the Church had not until then committed her authority to affirm this fact dogmatically. But that truth was already contained in God's Revelation, rather than added to it later on. Long before it was promulgated as a dogma, the divine Motherhood existed as a fact, from the instant when the Blessed Virgin Mary had answered 'Yes' to the Archangel Gabriel at her Annunciation. The dogmatic promulgation at Ephesus did not create the fact. It only provided formal assurance of orthodoxy. For this, the inhabitants of Ephesus in thanksgiving took to the streets, holding torches and singing hymns. Believers of all ages may react similarly when further aspects of God's Revelation are displayed by Holy Mother Church through her Magisterium.

GOD'S LOVE LETTER

God's Revelation is like his love letter to his immaculate Bride, the Church. For a letter to be safely transmitted, the sheet of paper requires folding into an envelope (or many sheets, because God has much to tell to his beloved). When a young woman receives a letter from her fiancé (ink on paper being more personal than emails on a screen or instant messages), she does not see the sentences and words, nor his handwriting and signature, until with her own fingers she delicately extracts the sheets from the envelope, and lovingly unfolds them for her eyes eventually to meet the written signs. Even then, although she can guess that he wrote gracious things about their shared love, she is not able to grasp in one glance the details of his communication. It takes unfolding and reading time — until the beloved returns.

With this comparison in mind, we may ask ourselves: what are the *fingers* with which Holy Mother Church unfolds God's message of love? They are the theologians and the Magisterium. The Church's *fingers* are Catholic believers of either sex mandated by the Holy See to apply their sound philosophical and theological training to probing Holy Scripture and Tradition. These people examine the Deposit of Faith according to their individual temperaments, skills and interests, seeking the guidance of the Holy Ghost and reacting to historical circumstances. In that sense, their inquiries entail novelty and subjectivity. But the object of their investigation can never be a product of their imagination, a fanciful innovation or an artificial addition, however clever or expedient it may sound. On the contrary, whatever they find has to be just that: *found* — not imagined. They can deduce, not invent.

Holy Mother Church, then, has loving fingers. Now, what is her love letter? Upon what sheet and within what sealed envelope did her beloved Jesus imprint his message of fervent love? It was upon a *burial* sheet, sealed within a stone cavity. On Easter morning, the risen Spouse let his angel break the seal from his tombstone; and his first pope found the empty shroud that covered the dead Lord's Holy Face and Body: *The napkin that had been about his head, [was] not lying with the linen cloths, but apart, wrapped up into one place* (Jn 20:7). Christ's message was folded, so that even Simon Peter did not behold the full silhouette of the Saviour at the time. Later on that memorable day however, the Vicar of Christ would have taken away with him for safekeeping the folded shroud — the material witness of the Resurrection, which is the core of the Christian Revelation as St Paul affirms: *If Christ be not risen again, then is our preaching vain, and your faith is also vain* (1 Cor 15:14).

TRUTH KNOWS NO EXPIRATION DATE

Certain dogmatic pronouncements can be more important than others, but they cannot contradict past ones. Some well-meaning Catholics believe, more or less consciously, that referring to Councils earlier than the twenty-first one (also the latest: Vatican II, 1962–1965) is disloyal. They mistakenly assume that what was defined in centuries past loses its relevance with time; or worse, that older truths become toxic after a number of years, like pharmaceutical drugs past expiration date. On 19th November 2013, Pope Francis proved such assumptions erroneous when he commemorated the 450th anniversary of the Council of Trent (1545–1563), writing to his extraordinary envoy Walter Cardinal Brandmüller:

> It behoves the Church to recall with more prompt and attentive eagerness the most fruitful doctrine which came out of that Council convened in the Tyrolese region. Certainly not without cause, the Church has for a long time already accorded so much care to the Decrees and Canons of that Council that are to be recalled and observed. . . . Graciously hearing the very same Holy Ghost, the Holy Church of our age, even now, continues to restore and meditate upon the most abundant doctrine of Trent. . . . You will exhort all who shall participate in this event, that, souls joined together with the soul of the Most Holy Redeemer, they may be fully conscious of all the fruits derived from this Council, and that they may unite themselves in bringing these fruits to others and in propagating them in every way.[2]

Thus, five centuries after the Council of Trent, the successor of Peter affirms the perennial validity of the truths defined in its documents, and commands them to be 'propagated in every way,' following Pope John Paul II's similar praise of 'the perennially valid teaching of the Council of Trent'.[3]

Still, it cannot be denied that of late, disconcerting statements have been issued by the hierarchy of the Church at every level. Even though no formal heresy has been promulgated, traditional teaching on marriage for instance, on death penalty or on the unicity and salvific universality of Jesus Christ and the Church, are being undermined. How are we clergy to react in such situations;

---

2   http://www.vatican.va/content/francesco/la/letters/2013/documents/papa-francesco_20131119_brandmuller-450-chiusura-concilio-trento.html, accessed 1st June 2020.

3   *Ecclesia de Eucharistia* §15, 17 April 2003.

how to guide our flock in peace and safety?

About the laity, the Code of Canon Law (1983) states that:

> They have the right, indeed at times the duty, in keeping
> with their knowledge, competence and position, to man-
> ifest to the sacred Pastors their views on matters which
> concern the good of the Church. They have the right
> also to make their views known to others of Christ's
> faithful, but in doing so they must always respect the
> integrity of faith and morals, show due reverence to the
> Pastors and take into account both the common good
> and the dignity of individuals (Can. 212 §3).

THE SENSE OF FAITH EQUIPS US TO DISCERN

A document of particular relevance to this question, *The Sense of
Faith in the Life of the Church*, was published under Pope Francis
by the International Theological Commission of the Holy See on
10th June 2014, explaining how the 'sense of faith' (in Latin *sensus
fidei*) enables the baptised to assess doctrinal truth. Here are six
important paragraphs from this document:

> 49. The *sensus fidei fidelis* is a sort of spiritual instinct
> that enables the believer to judge spontaneously whether
> a particular teaching or practice is or is not in con-
> formity with the Gospel and with apostolic faith. It is
> intrinsically linked to the virtue of faith itself; it flows
> from, and is a property of, faith. It is compared to an
> instinct because it is not primarily the result of rational
> deliberation, but is rather a form of spontaneous and
> natural knowledge, a sort of perception (*aisthesis*).
>
> 53. The *sensus fidei* is the form that the instinct which
> accompanies every virtue takes in the case of the virtue
> of faith. 'Just as, by the habits of the other virtues, one
> sees what is becoming in respect of that habit, so, by the
> habit of faith, the human mind is directed to assent to
> such things as are becoming to a right faith, and not to

assent to others.' Faith, as a theological virtue, enables the believer to participate in the knowledge that God has of himself and of all things. In the believer, it takes the form of a 'second nature.' By means of grace and the theological virtues, believers become 'participants of the divine nature' (2 Pet 1:4), and are in a way connaturalised to God. As a result, they react spontaneously on the basis of that participated divine nature, in the same way that living beings react instinctively to what does or does not suit their nature.

60. Three principal manifestations of the *sensus fidei fidelis* in the personal life of the believer can be highlighted. The *sensus fidei fidelis* enables individual believers: 1) to discern whether or not a particular teaching or practice that they actually encounter in the Church is coherent with the true faith by which they live in the communion of the Church (see below, §§ 61-63); 2) to distinguish in what is preached between the essential and the secondary (§ 64); and 3) to determine and put into practice the witness to Jesus Christ that they should give in the particular historical and cultural context in which they live (§ 65).

61. 'Beloved, do not believe every spirit, but test the spirits to see whether they are from God ; for many false prophets have gone out into the world' (1 Jn 4:1). The *sensus fidei fidelis* confers on the believer the capacity to discern whether or not a teaching or practice is coherent with the true faith by which he or she already lives. If individual believers perceive or 'sense' that coherence, they spontaneously give their interior adherence to those teachings or engage personally in the practices, whether it is a matter of truths already explicitly taught or of truths not yet explicitly taught.

62. The *sensus fidei fidelis* also enables individual believers to perceive any disharmony, incoherence, or contradiction between a teaching or practice and the

authentic Christian faith by which they live. They react as a music lover does to false notes in the performance of a piece of music. In such cases, believers interiorly resist the teachings or practices concerned and do not accept them or participate in them. 'The *habitus* of faith possesses a capacity whereby, thanks to it, the believer is prevented from giving assent to what is contrary to the faith, just as chastity gives protection with regard to whatever is contrary to chastity.'

63. Alerted by their *sensus fidei*, individual believers may deny assent even to the teaching of legitimate pastors if they do not recognise in that teaching the voice of Christ, the Good Shepherd. 'The sheep follow [the Good Shepherd] because they know his voice. They will not follow a stranger, but they will run away from him because they do not know the voice of strangers' (Jn 10:4-5). For St Thomas, a believer, even without theological competence, can and even must resist, by virtue of the *sensus fidei*, his or her bishop if the latter preaches heterodoxy. In such a case, the believer does not treat himself or herself as the ultimate criterion of the truth of faith, but rather, faced with materially 'authorised' preaching which he or she finds troubling, without being able to explain exactly why, defers assent and appeals interiorly to the superior authority of the universal Church.

FILIAL CONCERN

These authoritative quotes from a theological document published by the Holy See as recently as 2014 may surprise us for their boldness. They stress clearly that the undiscriminating acceptance of any doctrine, simply because a cleric proclaims it, is not Catholic. On the contrary, genuine worship of Christ as Truth Incarnate leads every believer to assess what is presented as truth, even when uttered by those acting in Christ's name. The touchstone of orthodoxy is continuity with what has always and everywhere been professed and believed in the Church of Christ:

> For the Holy Spirit was promised to the successors of
> Peter not so that they might, by his revelation, make
> known some new doctrine, but that, by his assistance,
> they might religiously guard and faithfully expound the
> revelation or deposit of faith transmitted by the apostles.[4]

With this in mind, one understands how considering the
hypothesis even of a heretical pope is not in itself imprudent or
disrespectful. Eminent and saintly theologians have done so, for
the sake of guiding souls in times of perplexity. Cardinal St Robert
Bellarmine stated that: *A Pope who is a manifest heretic, ceases in
himself to be Pope and head, just as he ceases in himself to be a
Christian and member of the body of the Church.*[5] It is one thing
for a sovereign pontiff to allow the spread of falsity by other prel-
ates, or even to support it privately, or to be quoted as such — it
is another for him to teach formal heresy with all the marks of
authority required to bind the Church to his error. St Bellarmine
believed that Christ would preserve his Church from the latter evil.

We clergy should all filially pray for this, while making better use of the wealth of safe doctrinal resources provided on the
Internet. At the tips of our fingers, we can gain access for free
to the texts of the twenty-one Councils and of numerous papal
encyclicals, but also of the Fathers of the Church and the works
of sound theologians and spiritual authors. All these doctrinal
riches are offered us as the gradual unfolding of Christ's revelation.
Nothing can be changed or added to Christ's Revelation, since it
was completed at the death of his last apostle St John the Evangelist (around 100 A D, in Ephesus). But much can be deduced from
the same revelation, through the humble and loving process of
explicating pre-existing truth, according to our analogy with the
unfolding of Christ's Holy Shroud.

As our reader may have noticed, bringing together Christ's Revelation and Shroud rests upon a motive stronger than an analogy.

---

4   Vatican I, *Pastor Aeternus*, Chapter 4.
5   *De Romano Pontifice*, lib. II, cap. 30.

The Shroud indeed bears witness to the Revelation in the most real-istic manner. It is significant that Easter Saturday's Gospel quoted above shows St John waiting outside the tomb for St Peter to enter first. Again, the respective positions of the linens are noticed as if through St Peter's eyes. Who more than Christ's Vicar has authority to guard, pass on and expound the treasure given by the Risen Lord? On that same Easter day, as we learn, the Lord 'appeared to Simon' (Lk 24:34). There were no witnesses. Or perhaps, the Shroud was the witness, as we now attempt to depict, offering this meditation to conclude our essay.

Alone at last in the Upper Room, Simon unfolded the long strip of cloth, nowhere more fittingly than across the trestles of the Last Supper table. Three nights earlier, upon another cloth, the Lord had made Himself truly present under the Eucharistic species at the first Holy Mass. The Eleven and He had walked thence to Gethsemane. Before cockcrow, Simon had thrice denied his Lord. Since then Jesus had died and was risen.

Back in the Upper Room on Easter day, Simon was on his knees at the far end of the long narrow linen rectangle. His eyes slightly higher than the level of the cloth swollen in successive waves upon the trestles, the fisherman looked at the maculated Shroud as a seaman at a vast archipelago spread across a limit-less map. Wide or tiny, each bloodstain was an island, mystically bearing the name of each and every sinner, redeemed through the wounds of the Lamb.

Which stain bore Simon's name? It couldn't be less than three, one for each denial—and so many more.... In St Peter's soul, contrition connected the reddish shapes of various sizes like the stars under which he was reborn, as in a new constellation named *Absolution*. It was probably no surprise to Simon then, when he became aware of Christ's bodily presence, standing at the other end of his unfolded Shroud. The contrite Vicar had opened his soul to the Saviour already. Christ confirmed his pardon and left, until they met again by the Sea of Galilee.

His Vicar remained on his knees looking across the bloodied sheet. On either side of that table of redemption hundreds of men would assemble, imitating his posture, Peter might have foreseen: his successors. What were their names, their races and languages: Clement, Anaclet, Alexander, Fabian, John, Stephen, Pius, Leo, Gregory, Benedict . . . Francis? How many of them would the Fisherman have until Christ's glorious return? The Lord would not fail to assist them, as he had done for him, that each might be faithful: *But I have prayed for thee, that thy faith fail not: and thou, being once converted, confirm thy brethren* (Lk 22:32).

Simon prayed for them, that they might 'feed Christ's sheep' (Jn 21:17) in the pastures of unadulterated truth, whatever the cost. In order to save though, truth must not only be believed, but also implemented by all believers. Every genuine Pope to Christ's flock would also have to 'teach them to observe all things whatsoever [the Lord had] commanded His apostles' (Mt 28:20). The Mother of the Lord had ordered it so, at the wedding in Cana. She did not command merely to *believe* whatever Christ would say, but to *do* it: *His mother saith to the waiters: Whatsoever he shall say to you, do ye* (Jn 2:5).

Presently, Peter felt her hand gently resting on his shoulder. No nail had pierced that hand, but a sword had pierced the immaculate heart of the Mother who, standing behind him, silently assured forgiveness to the kneeling penitent, and promised assistance to her Son's first Pope, now rising. Within fifty days, she would be with Peter and the ten others in this very room, when the Holy Ghost would be sent upon them, turning every believer into an 'epistle of Christ . . . written not with ink, but with the Spirit of the living God; not in tables of stone, but in the fleshly tables of the heart' (2 Cor 3:3).

How long would the unfolding of Christ's revelation take, until his return in might and glory? A few years; a few centuries; or millennia? One thing was certain: all that was ever to be proclaimed through dogmatic promulgations in the ages to come was already lying there, before Simon's tearful eyes, spread across the linen cloth of the Risen One. His message was imprinted on his Shroud: apparently flat, but unfathomably deep if measured in mercy—high as the heavens if measured by joy.

6

Priestly Unity and Concelebration

THE CHURCH PROCEEDS FROM THE EUCHARIST,
Pope John-Paul II reminded us in his key encyclical *Ecclesia de Eucharistia*.[1] Unity among all the baptised stems from the Holy Eucharist. This applies even more to the hierarchy of the Church, bishops, priests and all clergy. Thus, in this chapter we will examine how Eucharistic unity applies to clerics in particular. How does the Holy Eucharist foster unity among priests as ordained members of the Church? Most priests and laity would answer, in the Latin Church at least, that Eucharistic concelebration is the main expression of priestly unity. To help us examine this assumption, we will refer to the book *The Holy Eucharist—The World's Salvation* written in 1982 by Fr Joseph de Sainte-Marie, a French Carmelite friar, and published in English by Gracewing in 2015 with a preface by Dom Alcuin Reid OSB, a well-known liturgical scholar. Notably, Fr Joseph de Sainte-Marie was a daily celebrant of the Novus Ordo Missae, so that he cannot be suspected of partiality. He reflects on concelebration from a historical and theological perspective more than a liturgical one.

THE HOLY ANGELS CONCELEBRATE

In the Common Preface of the Roman Missal, before the *Sanctus*, the priest celebrant reads or sings to God the Father the following words about his Son Jesus Christ: *Through Whom the Angels praise Thy Majesty, Dominations worship, Powers stand in awe. The Heavens and the Heavenly hosts together with the blessed Seraphim in triumphant chorus unite to celebrate it*—or in Latin, *Per quem maiestatem tuam laudant Angeli, adorant dominationes, tremunt*

---

1   Released on April 17, 2003.

potestates. Caeli caelorumque virtutes, ac beata Seraphim socia exul-
tatione concelebrant. Then comes the *Sanctus*, that is, the angelic
choirs welcoming the Lamb of God on his way to the sacrifice,
'Holy, holy, holy Lord, God of hosts, heaven and earth are full of
your glory, hosanna in the highest.' The Latin expression is relevant
to our topic: *beata Seraphim socia exultatione concelebrant.* The
angels *concelebrate.* The verb 'to concelebrate' is used in a very
traditional sense here in reference to the angelic participation in
the sacrifice of the Mass.

The holy angels do not attend from a distance. Rather, they are
involved in a structured and ordered praise, shared with that of
the priest celebrant, the human beings physically present in the
church when the Holy Sacrifice is being offered, and the added
praise of all the others for whom the sacrifice is offered, such as the
holy souls in purgatory, or people who are alive on earth but not
physically present in the church. How striking to realise that the
verb 'to concelebrate' in its traditional meaning associates invisible
persons, angelic ones in this case. Concelebration, then, does not
require that one should be holding the bread and wine: since the
angels are not, the holy souls are not, and the congregation is not
holding anything else than hymnbooks or hand missals. Thus, we
recognize that the concept of concelebration is traditionally much
broader than what it has come to mean in recent decades.

THREE HISTORICAL MEANINGS OF CONCELEBRATION

A historical summary of concelebration distinguishes three
meanings according to the type of persons engaged.

1) **General concelebration.** The broader meaning is called 'general concelebration.' It involves the people in the pews as well as the
holy angels, the holy souls and the living uniting from a distance
with the offering of Holy Mass (including through a live Internet
broadcast).[2] They concelebrate with the priest because they join in.
Some are present in the church where they came of their own free

---

2   We recommend the excellent www.livemass.net, with its associated
phone application and up-to-date interactive map.

will. If not corporally present, as for angels or for a bed-ridden parishioner hearing the bell of consecration at her nearby parish church for instance, still, their intellect and will focus on the action being offered. This concelebration could be called 'general' because it involves the whole Church.

2) **Ceremonial concelebration.** The second meaning of concelebration is a bit narrower in scope, applying to ordained ministers and called 'ceremonial concelebration.' This ceremonial concelebration involves more than only the priest and deacon. Traditionally indeed, preparation for the priesthood encompasses various stages, as is still the case at a seminary like the one where the author was formed in Wigratzbad, Germany, or Our Lady of Guadalupe Seminary in the United States (Denton, Nebraska).[3] One begins with clerical tonsure early in the second year. From that moment, one becomes liturgically a cleric.[4] In that capacity one starts wearing the cassock and is enabled to perform certain functions proper to clerics. One is already consecrated. For instance, whereas in the first year one would wear gloves when touching the *empty* sacred vessels in the sacristy to set a chalice for the priest, from the time when one is tonsured, one does not wear gloves anymore. Instead, one may touch the (empty) sacred vessels with bare hands because one has been consecrated during the ceremony of Tonsure, when the bishop symbolically cut five locks of hair from the candidate's head. As explained earlier, the four minor orders follow, namely

3 At each of these two international seminaries, about eighty seminarians from various countries follow the traditional seven-year curriculum. Our Lady of Guadalupe Seminary is so far the only traditional seminary in the world forming English-speaking candidates in full communion with the Church: www.fsspolgs.org. The seminary also offers training sessions and retreats for diocesan priests.

4 In 1983, Pope John Paul II's new Code of Canon Law postponed the admission into the canonical state to the reception of the order of the diaconate. This made sense since Tonsure, Minor Orders and the major Order of the Subdiaconate had been suppressed by Pope Paul VI in the early 1970s. Since 1988 though, by acknowledgement of the Holy See, they are part of the discipline proper to the Priestly Fraternity of St Peter and of other subsequently founded communities.

Porter, Lector, Exorcist and Acolyte. Each of these steps is an actual ordination, minor indeed, but real, which further empowers the young cleric to perform certain functions, always in connection with the Sacred Mysteries. These four lower steps are mirrored by the four major orders: Subdiaconate, Diaconate, Presbyterate, and Episcopate. What a beautiful symmetry between these four minor and four major orders!

Thus, *ceremonial* concelebration involves these various clerics in the performing of the sacred action, each one according to his proper rank and order. Notably, not every minister of the same rank will do the same thing at the same time. *Ceremonial* concelebration brings together all these ministers as doing *different* things at the same time within the same Holy Mass. Their combined actions bring to completion and to fullness the sacred ceremony. It could be compared to an orchestra, where each musician plays his own instrument, following his own melody, not as if ignoring the others, but on the contrary, enhancing unity through the display of ordered diversity. Even though a cellist might also be an excellent flutist, for the duration of the performance, he acts as cellist only.

As we can see, *ceremonial* concelebration is about complementarity. Each minister brings to the action something which the other cannot bring, either because he has not received that order yet; or if he has, because he is presently performing a function proper to another rank. For instance, an ordained priest acting as acolyte at a Mass will not therefore transubstantiate on that occasion. Or if he is a deacon, he might be acting as subdeacon only, hence not singing the gospel. This is striking at traditional priestly gatherings, when a solemn high Mass may be offered during which every lower function is also fulfilled by a priest: not only those of deacon and subdeacon, but even of acolytes, Master of Ceremonies, thurifer and (incense) boat bearer. At a higher level, in Rome even bishops used to act as bearers of liturgical items at the traditional papal Mass, plainly sitting on the altar steps when the pontiff preached, like mere altar boys. How humbling, and hence edifying. Concelebrating ceremonially also emphasizes the intrinsic dignity of the Holy Sacrifice as Christ's own action, in which ordained ministers from Porter to Bishop act only in the person and name of Christ. Consequently, no function is to be considered below one's rank. Fulfilling lower roles is an honour, no less than higher ones, because all are part of the one sacrifice of Christ. Such is the beautiful variety and orderliness of the *ceremonial* concelebration.

3) **Sacramental concelebration.** After the concelebration in a *general* sense, and following our presentation of *ceremonial* concelebration, let us now consider *sacramental* concelebration. This third type of concelebration seems to be the only one envisaged in modern times. When without further qualifiers a priest says: 'I concelebrated the 9am Mass this morning,' what is meant is *sacramental* concelebration. The meaning of the word 'concelebrating' has been *de facto* narrowed to what is in fact a very limited understanding of the word according to Catholic tradition. *Sacramental* concelebration refers to two or more priests transubstantiating bread and wine into the Body and Blood of the Lord, uttering together the two formulas of Eucharistic consecration. In fact, concelebrating in the modern sense means *co-transubstantiating* (if one dares add yet a third prefix to *trans-* and *sub-*). Modern or *sacramental* concelebration is about several presbyters performing the change of bread and wine into the Body and Blood of Christ at the same time.

How surprising then to learn from Dom Alcuin Read's preface to Joseph de St Marie's work that, based on historical evidence, the type of concelebration which has always been in use in the Church is *not* the *sacramental* one, but the *ceremonial* one. When priests and bishops were concelebrating, roughly up to Vatican II, what was meant and what was happening was not transubstantiating together. There was only one minister transubstantiating, while all others were associated in his action ceremonially, as we have described earlier. In other words, if some of these ministers were ordained priests rather than only deacons, or subdeacons, or acolytes, etc, if they were priests, by the end of such concelebration in its traditional understanding, these other ministers would not have offered Mass in their own right. They would have concelebrated

it ceremonially, but they would not have been, each of them, the
ministerial instrument through which transubstantiation occurred.
Concelebration traditionally understood would have been very
rarely sacramental concelebration. When it did happen on special
occasions, concelebration would normally have been *ceremonial*.
Because this important topic deserves a much broader treatment
than we can offer in the present chapter, we recommend reading *The Holy Eucharist—The World's Salvation* by Fr Joseph de
Sainte-Marie.

AROUND THE BISHOP

Not only did traditional concelebration require one celebrant
only, in addition he had to be the local bishop. This expresses
the traditional understanding of Holy Mass as restoring a *vertical*
relationship between fallen man and God through the sacrifice of
Christ on the Cross; Holy Mass being the unbloody re-presentation
of the sacrifice at Golgotha. Unlike priests, deacons and lower
ministers, the bishop has the fullness of the priesthood, whereby
he embodies Christ and offers the Divine Victim *in persona Christi*.
On the contrary, all lower ministers act by the delegation and permission[5] of the bishop, sharing and helping in the sacred action
at a subordinate level, a bit like the branches in relation to the
trunk. This is manifest in the traditional form at an ordination
ceremony or a pontifical Holy Mass. Then, the vesting of the pontiff
is performed as a rite in itself, whether in the sacristy or even at
the altar. The bishop puts on one layer upon the other, like the
various orders he recapitulates: upon the amice and alb he dons
the tunic of the subdeacon, the dalmatic of the deacon and finally
the chasuble of the priest. This is a vestimentary display of the
fullness of orders received by the bishop. The ministers of lower
ranks concelebrate the sacred action ceremonially according to the
hierarchy of orders. Such traditional concelebration is hierarchical,

---

5   Even though they permanently retain a sharing in Christ's priesthood,
by virtue of the rite of ordination received. Priests in particular never lose
their God-given power to offer Holy Mass.

revolving around the person of the bishop who embodies Christ in his diocese, i.e. the local Church. This is the way even diocesan Chrism Masses used to be conducted, as has been now resumed for example in the Archdiocese of Vaduz in Liechtenstein since 2013.

THEOLOGICAL PRINCIPLES

Holy Church wants many Holy Masses. A key question about concelebration is the number of Holy Masses being offered. Is there only one Holy Mass offered or, as many Holy Masses as there are concelebrants? We now speak of the *sacramental* concelebration in the modern understanding. Does the number of Masses offered matter? Yes, because the Church wants the multiplication of Holy Masses, as Father Joseph de Sainte-Marie explains:

'Every time that the memory of this Sacrifice is cele-brated, the work of our redemption is wrought.' It can be said that Paul VI and Vatican II only drew, or rather recalled, the practical consequences of this doctrine when, in basing themselves explicitly on it, they invited priests to celebrate Mass daily. On 3rd September 1965, in his encyclical *Mysterium Fidei*, Paul VI stated the following: 'The Mass, even if it is celebrated individually by one priest, is not therefore private, but it is the action of Christ and of the Church. This latter has learned to offer itself, in the sacrifice which it offers, in a universal sacrifice, applying to the salvation of the entire world the redemptive, unique and infinite power of the sacrifice of the Cross. Every Mass is, in fact, offered not only for the salvation of some individuals, but for the salvation of the entire world. . . . This is why,' Paul VI continues, '. . . We recommend with a paternal insistence that priests, who in a special way are Our joy and crown in the Lord, cel-ebrate the Mass each day, with all dignity and devotion.'[6]

6   Sainte-Marie, Joseph de, *The Holy Eucharist — The World's Salvation* (Leominster: Gracewing, 2015), 306–07.

Father Joseph de Sainte-Marie continues:

> 'On the 6th of December in that same year, citing in a
> footnote these words of Paul VI, the Council solemnly
> continued the exhortation, in its Decree on the Ministry
> and Life of Priests: "In the mystery of the Eucharistic
> sacrifice, where priests exercise their special function,
> it is the work of our redemption which is unceasingly
> accomplished." This is why they are highly recom-
> mended to celebrate the Mass every day; even if the
> Christian faithful cannot be present, it is an act of Christ
> and of the Church."'

This quote is from *Presbyterorum Ordinis* (#13), an official
document of the Second Vatican Council. It shows that even the
recent Magisterium of the Church continues to recommend, if not
to *demand* the daily celebration of Holy Mass. Why is this? The
quote from *Presbyterorum Ordinis*, which has appeared in many
other documents like *Mediator Dei* of Pius XII in 1947, is in fact
the Secret of the traditional Roman Missal under the ninth Sunday after Pentecost: *Grant us, we beseech You, O Lord, to worthily
frequent these sacred mysteries: for as often as this saving victim is
offered up, so often is furthered the work of our redemption.* Or in
Latin, *Concéde nobis, quæsumus, Domine, hæc digne frequentare
mysteria: quia, quoties huius hostiæ commemoratio celebratur, opus
nostræ redemptionis exercetur.* Let us explain an important distinction which is at stake here.

Acquisition and application of Christ's merits. Christians profess that salvation comes from the saving merits of Christ, the only
Saviour. But some faithful and even perhaps some priests may not
recall that this truth includes two different stages. The first stage
is about Christ acquiring the merits to save us. It occurred only
once, when Our Lord died on the cross at 3pm, on Mount Golgotha,
outside of Jerusalem, in the year 33. This first stage considers the
acquisition of all saving merits by the sinless Christ on behalf of
all sinners. But a second stage must follow, namely, the *application*

of the same saving merits to sinners. This application of the merits occurs all throughout human history (i.e., the history of the Church since Pentecost) whenever men and women willingly and knowingly open their souls to Christ, requesting spiritual cleansing. With contrition, in response to God's grace, penitents pray, learn their faith, receive sacramentals (such as medals, scapulars, holy water or the sign of the cross) and the seven sacraments of the Church, culminating in the Holy Sacrifice of the Mass.

In other words, the saving merits of Christ are absolutely necessary for salvation. But once acquired by Our Lord on the cross, they need to be applied to souls in the succession of ages and the diversity of places. And this application is achieved essentially in the offering of Holy Mass. Thus, the merits once acquired must then be applied, since 'God who created us without us, does not want to save us without us' — as Saint Augustine wrote.[7] Human creatures can be saved because unlike animals they are endowed with reason and free will. Angels also have reason and free will but, unlike humans, they cannot err or repent, therefore salvation doesn't apply to them. We cannot be saved against our will. We need to respond 'Yes' to grace, a genuinely free 'Yes' to God who offers us salvation. Being the application of the saving merits of Christ to the wounds of our souls, which are our sins, this stage two is precisely the opportunity granted us by God to answer 'Yes.' When a layman feels tired on a rainy morning and still gets out of bed and walks to a weekday Mass at the local parish on his way to work, he achieves something very meritorious. He is telling Christ, 'Sweet Jesus, my beloved Saviour, I know that you acquired these saving merits once and forever on the cross on my behalf. But I also know that you will not force them upon me. This is why I come to you on this (rainy) morning of my own free will to kneel at your altar rail, begging you to cleanse my soul with your saving blood through your Holy Eucharist.'

When considering Christ's merits, distinguishing always between these two stages of acquisition and application is essential.

7 Quoted by CCC #1847.

Obviously they are connected, but distinct. Once again, all Christians profess that only the saving merits of Christ can reconcile us with God, setting us free from the devil. But if acquired by Christ once and for all on the cross, these saving merits further require application to souls in the diversity of times and places.

How many Holy Masses per concelebration? Let us come back to the traditional Secret of the ninth Sunday after Pentecost quoted by Pope Paul VI and by Vatican II, 'For as often as this saving victim is offered up, so often is furthered the work of our redemption.' It explains why Holy Mother Church, passionately in love with her Divine Bridegroom our Lord, and maternally caring for us her children, wants the multiplication of Holy Masses. This is the key to our present consideration. It helps us look again at the question of *sacramental* concelebration as understood in the modern way. Is there one Mass offered or as many Masses as concelebrating priests? If there is one Mass offered in total, there are as many Masses not taking place as there are concelebrants. This means that there are as many failed applications of the saving merits of Christ to the needs of souls. On the contrary, if there are as many Masses offered as there are concelebrating priests, souls are not deprived. According to that hypothesis, if for instance one hundred priests concelebrate (sacramentally), one hundred Holy Masses are offered (by them simultaneously). But in the opposite hypothesis, if one hundred concelebrants offer one single Holy Mass so that ninety-nine Holy Masses are not said, then ninety-nine applications of the saving merits of Christ to souls are missed.

Based on sound theology and history, and in harmony with the relevant Church Magisterium,[8] the answer given by Fr Joseph de Sainte-Marie is that one Holy Mass only is offered at any sacramental concelebration.[9] This is the case whether the concelebrants are two or three, or several thousand, as at World Youth Days. We

8   A philosophical and theological study of this question by the Holy See followed by an official conclusion would help bishops, priests and the laity immensely.

9   However, each concelebrant has really offered holy Mass, which entitles him to a separate Mass stipend.

should not be afraid of pondering these matters. Concelebration in itself, even sacramental, is not something wrong. If the Church were obsessed with multiplying the number of Holy Masses, she would have allowed every priest to offer Mass more than once a day, as a matter of principle rather than of exception as stated in the 1983 Code of Canon Law: *A priest is not permitted to celebrate the Eucharist more than once a day except in cases where the law permits him to celebrate or concelebrate more than once on the same day* (Canon 905).

Binating[10] is allowed upon permission sought and granted. If the Church wanted a sheer multiplication of Holy Masses, she would have commanded her priests to offer Holy Mass twelve times a day, or more. But this is not the case, as we know. Holy Mother Church acts with propriety, proportion, balance and common sense. She approves of priests celebrating the Holy Sacrifice in common for a just cause, even though this makes them less likely to offer Mass separately that day, thus reducing the amount of graces released upon the world. In consequence, to concelebrate sacramentally is not something wrong *per se*. In fact, the same conclusion could apply to *ceremonial* concelebration, when on certain occasion priests may choose not to offer Mass elsewhere but to act instead as deacon, subdeacon or some lower order at a Solemn or Pontifical High Mass. (However, our experience is that priests formed in a traditional way would always offer Mass individually on the same day, before or after concelebrating ceremonially.) The principle of concelebration is not at stake but its extension, its mode and all the circumstances which, particularly over the past few decades, seem to change the perception of what it means to celebrate Mass. Misunderstanding the nature and purpose of Holy Mass and of the sacred priesthood is the problem, not concelebration in itself. Let us mention succinctly some of the risks incurred when sacramental concelebration becomes *de facto* the norm, while Holy Mass offered by one celebrant is only an exception.

---

10   To binate is to offer two holy Masses within a day; to trinate is offering three holy Masses on the same day.

SIX RISKS INCURRED BY SYSTEMATIC SACRAMENTAL CONCELEBRATION

1) The first risk is of being denied the celebration of Holy Mass as a single celebrant (we could call this *monocelebration*). Many priests have had such unpleasant experiences when travelling or on pilgrimage. Understandably their visit as fellow priests may not have been included in the schedule of that parish, because the priest in charge could be informed only too late. The latter sometimes refuses an altar to his visitor on the grounds that this extra Mass was not announced in the bulletin, offering instead to concelebrate at the time scheduled.

On the contrary, the Second Vatican Council states that 'each priest shall always retain his right to celebrate Mass individually' (*Sacrosanctum Concilium* #57, 2). Needless to say, this right to offering Holy Mass as sole celebrant can only be urged with courtesy and common sense, not at the same time as another concelebration or of planned activities taking place in the same church such as rehearsals, cleaning and public devotions. No visiting priest with good sense would demand that an altar should be set for him the minute he arrives. Rather, he would express his petition to the local priest or his representative with humility, patience and charity, saying for instance: *Good morning Father. I am Fr Smith and this is my celebret.*[11] *As per my email two weeks ago, I am here on holiday and, at whatever time is suitable for you, I will be grateful to have access to one of the altars in your church to offer Holy Mass. I have brought along with me some items you may not have at hand, including my linens.*

2) When fellow priests are repeatedly denied their right to offer Holy Mass singly, they risk giving up. They will not bother anymore pleading for their daily Mass. When travelling or on holiday, they may end up thinking, *Look, I'm tired; I'm on holiday; I'm not going*

---

11   The *celebret* (a Latin word meaning 'let him celebrate' Mass) is the ecclesiastical identity card of a priest. Normally displaying the name, surname, picture, date of birth and diocese of the bearer, the celebret is issued every year by the priest's bishop or religious superior to demonstrate priestly identity and good standing.

there to fight, but to rest. I find it demanding enough for me to set time aside just for a daily Mass with no one attending, bringing along on the plane my missal in case they don't have one in my language, and my alb and linens to save their sacristan work. But I was denied an altar once, twice, thrice and now it's over. I'm fed up. So might think or speak a disheartened priest. He may add, *I will take a little bag along with me with a few liturgical items. If I have a sense that I'm going to be welcomed, or if the parish there has a better reputation, or if I know the local priest well, then I will offer Mass singly; but otherwise I won't bother. I tried in my hotel room, but the TV screen took too much space on the chest-of-drawers and the whole experience felt awkward. I go there to relax, not to start a war or to minister underground. And that's the end of it.* This is how many priests end up, while travelling, or on holiday, or on other occasions, to simply not even ask for offering Holy Mass on certain days.

3) This in turn leads to overlooking the importance of offering Holy Mass singly, to the expense of one's priestly identity as Fr Joseph de Sainte-Marie eloquently describes:

> If concelebration indisputably reinforces... the senti-
> ment of belonging to a community, it no less deprives
> the priest of a quantity of gestures and words, which
> come down to him as his right or priority: to say the
> prayers of the Church, to read the Word of God, to offer
> the oblations placed on the altar, to give thanks after
> Communion in the name of the people, to bless, etc. In
> place of this, when he concelebrates, he responds to the
> prayers of the principal celebrant, like all the other peo-
> ple assisting; he listens to the readings (often done by
> a layman); he frequently presents the oblations, called
> 'gifts,' to the same principal celebrant (whereas this is
> a gesture proper to the laity); he receives Communion,
> the final blessing, etc.[12]

---

12 Sainte-Marie, *The Holy Eucharist — The World's Salvation*, 114–15.

4) Another risk occasioned by systematic concelebration is more likely to affect the laity. It consists of a Protestant misunderstanding of the priestly identity, especially as regards the power to transubstantiate. Visually speaking, many Catholic faithful experience Holy Mass nearly always as offered by a group spread around the altar. Some members of the group happen to be ordained ministers, while on the other side of the altar stand other members of the group, the non-ordained baptised. In such a setting, the people's perception is likely to shift, gradually and without any ill will, to a Protestant understanding of how the Eucharistic Presence might occur. It could suggest that not only the priest(s) but the overall worshipping community somehow, through its faith and desire, makes the Eucharistic Presence occur. The essential distinction between 'ministerial priesthood' and 'common priesthood' might become blurred.[13] This would contradict the teaching of the Church, which affirms that the ministerial priesthood of those ordained and the common priesthood of the baptised faithful 'differ from one another in essence and not only in degree.'[14] It becomes less clear that the ordained priest, and only him, brings about the Eucharistic presence so that, were he surrounded by one thousand Calvinists or by one thousand Catherine of Sienas, transubstantiation would occur all the same, regardless of the faith and dispositions of the persons present. Admittedly, the people's participation into the sacred action through intellect and will is required for them to merit. But the actual effect, the transubstantiation, is brought about by the priest celebrant alone, not in any sense by the people, irrespective of their greater or smaller number, faith or sanctity.

5) A further risk of lesser consequence is fuelling pride, as when one might boast of having had nine concelebrating priests at one's daughter's wedding, when one's niece had only three priests. One

13   Holy Church was compelled to warn against this tendency in her *Instruction On Certain Questions Regarding the Collaboration of the Non-Ordained Faithful In the Sacred Ministry As Priest*—15th August 1997 (www.vatican.va/roman_curia/congregations/cclergy/documents/rc_con_interdic_doc_15081997_en.html).

14   Vatican II, *Lumen Gentium*, chapter 2, #10.

might remark that, for one's father's funeral, one secured seven concelebrants whereas one's neighbour's funeral attracted only two priests. The number of concelebrants is easily turned into an indicator of the social importance of the event and of its lay actors. This is uncharitable towards less sought-after parishioners. It is also doctrinally erroneous, since each liturgical action is primarily an action of Christ and his Church, regardless of the number of associated ministers present.

6) Lastly, systematic concelebration threatens the spiritual needs of the people. In dioceses where parishes are being merged, Holy Mass does not take place in every former parish church any longer every Sunday (let alone every day). Instead, priests and laity from all across the new pastoral unit are expected to gather in one single different church every Sunday, according to a monthly or trimestrial rota, leaving the five, ten or twenty other churches without Sunday Mass. The laudable purpose is to muster all resources within one church at a time to give the impression of greater numbers and boost confidence. While this strategy might succeed for parishioners with a more flexible mindset (often the younger ones), it penalises those incapable of or unwilling to travel outside their original parish (often the older ones). It might be tempting to write off those as unavoidable casualties in the new policy dictated by the shortage of clergy and of parishioners. However, these more sedentary souls are long-time parishioners and still alive; whereas instead of concelebrating in one church, the several priests of the area could still offer Mass singly for the benefit of the less mobile members of the flock. As a result, many of those will simply stop going to Sunday Mass. Having lost that essential habit, they are even less likely to turn up in their local village church when a priest on holiday offers Mass there for the first time in months. Instead of slowing down decline in Mass attendance, concelebration in such situations accelerates lapsation.

SIGNS OF PRIESTLY UNITY

Concelebration is one option among many signs of sacramental unity. Any priest may legitimately abstain from concelebrating sacramentally, as the Second Vatican Council reminds us: '*Each*

priest shall always retain his right to celebrate Mass individually'
(*Sacrosanctum Concilium* #57, 2). Suspecting these priests of undermining the Eucharistic unity of the clergy would betray a superficial grasp of priestly identity and of Eucharistic doctrine. For
instance, the author once attended the Mass of installation of a
new bishop where the papal nuncio, an archbishop, participated in
choir dress, kneeling at a prie-dieu in the sanctuary. His reason for
not concelebrating was not ill-health; neither could it have been a
lack of orthodoxy. Rather, as the representative of the Sovereign
Pontiff, he would have had to be the main celebrant. Since the
new bishop was acting in that capacity, the nuncio participated
through prayer without concelebrating.

Admittedly, some priests may abstain for the wrong reasons if,
for instance, they find concelebration a clericalist practice which
'emphasizes the ministerial priesthood, belittling the laity.' On the
other hand, some healthily conservative diocesan priests sometimes
abstain from concelebrating at large diocesan functions when the
liturgy fails to meet the standards of decorum laid down by the
Church. Some non-diocesan priests readily pray together with the
bishop and fellow priests while abiding by the customs of their
own communities favouring ceremonial concelebration rather than
sacramental. They will attend Holy Mass in choir wearing cassock
and surplice (receiving Holy Communion on Maundy Thursday),
will take part in Eucharistic adoration with fellow clergy and will
join in the choral recitation of the Divine Office at deanery meetings or other clergy gatherings.

As an extension of the Eucharistic core of the priestly ministry,
sacramental unity with the bishop and fellow priests is also fostered
and manifested through the obtaining of faculties from the chief
pastor of the diocese or his delegate to administer the sacrament of
Penance validly; to witness wedding vows validly in the sacrament
of Matrimony; and to confer the sacrament of Confirmation by
delegation. Episcopal faculties must also be sought by priests to
lawfully offer Holy Mass, perform the sacrament of the Anointing
of the Sick and deliver homilies. The Holy Oils used in several
sacraments are consecrated by the bishop, whose power is thus

present everywhere and every time his priests baptise, confirm and anoint. In this very concrete way, each priest is conscious of the bond of sacramental communion with his bishop embodying Christ the Sovereign High Priest and chief Minister of every sacrament, and also with his fellow-priests.

Earlier expressions of priestly unity. Prior to the introduction of sacramental concelebration in the 1960s, the unity of priests with their bishop and among themselves was expressed through diverse signs and customs. Since the faith of the Church in general and the priestly identity in particular cannot change, these signs of unity retain their value for us today and provide inspiration.

A priest could not offer Holy Mass using a new chalice and paten until the bishop had consecrated them. This consecration was not a mere priestly blessing but a solemn rite described in the Roman Pontifical, performed by the bishop wearing his mitre and anointing the inside of the vessels with holy chrism. This rite sets the vessels apart for their exclusive use in immediate contact with the Eucharistic accidents[15] of bread and wine. Bringing the new vessels to the bishop for consecration is a very meaningful way of expressing Eucharistic unity with the chief pastor of the diocese.[16] Through the consecration of these quintessentially priestly items, the chalice and paten, the bishop becomes associated as instrumental cause with every Holy Mass subsequently offered with them. The episcopal consecration of the vessels makes their use lawful, as the mention of the bishop's name by the priest celebrant at the Canon of the Mass pertains to its licit celebration.

Because of their immediate connection with the sacrifice of the Mass, priestly vestments, altar cloths, corporals and purificators used to be blessed by the bishop also. For the same purpose of setting apart from worldly use, the ordaining bishop still anoints the palms of the ordinand with the oil of catechumens (or, for

15 The Eucharistic 'accidents' or 'externals' of bread and wine are treated with utter reverence as the ultimate 'vessels' of the substance of the Body and Precious Blood of the Lord, united with his human soul and divinity.

16 The author is glad to have done so with the bishops of the dioceses where he was successively assigned.

the consecration of a bishop, with holy chrism). The *Pontifical* listed also blessings to be imparted by the bishop to pyxes and monstrances. Despite their Eucharistic purpose, those latter vessels don't immediately pertain to the sacrifice of the Mass, hence they are not ritually *consecrated* but only blessed.

The older canonical discipline stressed the necessity of offering Holy Mass within a consecrated (Catholic) church building, and upon a consecrated altar.[17] While the phrasing of the liturgical law in force[18] is not significantly weaker than the old, its implementation has been dramatically defective. Since the 1960s, Holy Masses in great numbers have been offered outside sacred places; while inside churches, mere tables were and still are habitually used, that is, pieces of furniture bearing no consecration crosses in their corners and centre, never once anointed and blessed by the bishop, and not fixed to the floor. Instead of the relics of saints enshrined in altar stones, the only permanent feature of such Eucharistic tables is the microphone. By contrast, the altar stone expresses a vertical and supernatural communication between those present at the Holy Sacrifice of the Mass below, and the saints interceding for them from the celestial court on high. On the contrary, the microphone pertains to instantaneous and horizontal communication from the celebrant to the people in the pews. While microphones may be used upon an altar for convenience, swapping them with altar stones surely does not improve sacramental unity between the local community and the Mystical Body of Christ; rather, it cuts it off. Thankfully, priests careful to abide by the law and mind of the Church in these matters are genuine promoters of sacramental unity.

Until suppressed by Pope Paul VI in 1972, the clerical tonsure administered to the young seminarian by the bishop would be kept visible once he was ordained, marking the priest in the world as a minister of Christ under the bishop's protection. A bishop once told the author that he hoped that the ecclesiastical tonsure

---

17   Code of Canon Law of 1917, canon 822. Even in times of war or persecution, a consecrated altar stone was required (e.g. a light engraved slate).
18   Code of Canon Law of 1983, canon 932.

would be brought back, as it would allow him 'to see his priests wherever they are, even in a swimming pool.' While bishops of old would of course respect their priests' natural right to privacy, they would nonetheless be pleased to know that their priestly character was manifested externally in every circumstance as a reminder to priests and non-priests of the proper behaviour required by the divine mark in their soul. While ecclesiastical tonsure is not mandated any more, clerical attire is, as stressed by the *Directory on the Ministry and Life of Priests*: *Outside of entirely exceptional cases, a cleric's failure to use this proper ecclesiastical attire could manifest a weak sense of his identity as one consecrated to God.*[19] Wearing one's clericals even outside the church building strongly emphasizes one's priestly identity as shared with fellow priests across one's diocese, under the fatherly vigilance of the bishop.

United in Eucharistic faith, reverent worship and rubrical loyalty. Fundamentally, the unity of the Church rests upon the unity of faith, worship and government. For clergy, the unity of faith implies preaching all perennial truths in season and out of season. The unity of worship requires administering the seven sacraments of the Church and her sacramentals according to the rubrics proper to the diverse liturgical rites.[20] The unity of government demands obedience to the legitimate successor of the first pope St Peter and to the bishops united with him. These three blessed parameters

19   Cf. *Directory on the Ministry and Life of Priests*, Congregation for the Clergy, Copyright Libreria Editrice Vaticana, 31st January 1994, #66. *Obligation of Ecclesiastical Attire.*

20   Unity of worship must not be confused with *uniformity of rite*, as Joseph Cardinal Ratzinger explained in his October 24th, 1998 lecture on the Tenth anniversary of the Motu Proprio *Ecclesia Dei* in Rome: 'Several forms of the Latin rite have always existed, and were only slowly withdrawn, as a result of the coming together of the different parts of Europe. Before the Council there existed side by side with the Roman rite, the Ambrosian rite, the Mozarabic rite of Toledo, the rite of Braga, the Carthusian rite, the Carmelite rite, and best known of all, the Dominican rite, and perhaps still other rites of which I am not aware. No one was ever scandalized that the Dominicans, often present in our parishes, did not celebrate like diocesan priests but had their own rite. We did not have any doubt that their rite was as Catholic as the Roman rite, and we were proud of the richness inherent in these various traditions.'

of unity have been contested and ignored by some priests and bishops over the Church's twenty-century long history. Their faithful observance can be costly, while their absence sooner or later shows. Disunity about faith, worship and government should be remedied, not concealed.

One may then wonder whether in some occasions sacramental concelebration is not too minimal an expression of unity. Concelebration might conveniently dispense bishops and priests from mentioning the 'elephant in the room,' namely, disunity in doctrine, liturgy and law (including *moral* law). Such concelebrations conceal and thus perpetuate disunity, rather than foster unity. On the contrary, the more the triple fundament of Church unity is acknowledged by a bishop and his priests, the less sacramental concelebration appears as a *sine qua non* condition of unity. In such places, on special occasions, sacramental concelebration around the bishop in full respect of the rubrics and with diligent care of the sacred species is welcomed as one among various possible expressions of priestly unity.

THE IMPLICIT SHIFT FROM SACRAMENTAL TO CEREMONIAL CONCELEBRATION

1) Sensorial presence: To begin with, we suggest that examining the sensorial presence of concelebrants to the Eucharistic gifts enriches the perspective on this topic. The rubric of the Ordinary Form Roman Missal states that, *Each [concelebrant] extend[s] his right hand toward the bread and toward the chalice, if this seems appropriate; and at the elevation looking toward them and after this bowing profoundly.*[21] Concelebrants are not required to look at the gifts as they utter the Consecration formulas, but only after, when the sacred species are being elevated. Some concelebrants look at the gifts already during consecration, as is commendable. But it does happen though that priest concelebrants are prevented from seeing the bread and the wine on the altar because they stand too far away, like at World Youth Days; or simply because several

21   Cf. GIRM 222, 227, 230, 233.

dozens of priests stand between them and the altar, when at a diocesan event. Are then the bread and wine sensorially present to them? If these gifts lie beyond the range of his physical senses—especially his sight—is not the priest in a situation similar to some other priest who, possibly unwell, or mildly senile, or disabled, and in a wheelchair, unites from a distance without a definite intention to transubstantiate? Or else, should a special indult be granted to concelebrants prevented from seeing the gifts, as was the case for blind priests offering Holy Mass?[22] But because such blind priests consecrated individually rather than concelebrated, they would at least feel the bread with their fingers and smell the wine in the chalice with their nose, so that these gifts were sensorially present to them, albeit not visually. Such is not the case of concelebrants in good health, standing too far from the gifts. The importance of the issue calls for a clarification for the following reason.

If some concelebrants are not sensorially present to the gifts, a theological explanation is required to state how this obstacle does not affect their transubstantiating. When some of the concelebrants utter, '*This* is my Body' and '*This* is the chalice of my Blood,' while neither their eyes can see nor their fingers touch nor their nose smell bread and wine, what does the word '*This*' refer to? Or rather, since the word evidently is meant to refer to the gifts on the corporal, what distance is deemed sufficient to make consecration impossible? If a concelebrant arrives late and, out of discretion, remains in the pews during the Consecration while uttering the formulas with the intention to concelebrate,[23] will his words have effectuated transubstantiation, or not? Would it matter whether he stood on the edge of the sanctuary, or in the front pew, or further back—or even at the rear of the nave? Doesn't this raise serious questions about the nature of such concelebration? In other words, is it still a *sacramental* concelebration?

22   Cf. Instruction of the Congregation of Sacred Rites, dated April 15, 1961.

23   Such intention would of course contradict GIRM No. 206, stating that 'No one is ever to enter into a concelebration or to be admitted as a concelebrant once the Mass has already begun.' Unlawful as this priest's concelebration is, would it also be invalid?

For want of a magisterial statement on this issue, one may wonder whether in some cases, what is assumed to be a sacramental concelebration has not in fact shifted, more or less consciously, to a *ceremonial* concelebration. Could it not happen that some of the concelebrants standing in the sanctuary too far from the altar might be concelebrating in a ceremonial manner, even unknowingly? They would attend and participate with their heart but, even though they may utter the words of consecration, they might not really intend to transubstantiate;[24] or distance might invalidate their intention. Needless to say, these considerations are not included as a judgement on concelebrants, but merely as a reminder of classical distinctions to us all priests, for the good of the sacrament, of their recipients, and for our own good. Indeed this applies just as well to priests offering Holy Mass as sole celebrants. Any priest must have at least a *habitual* intention to consecrate when offering Holy Mass. He must want 'to do what

24   The following guidelines are offered in the Extraordinary Form Roman Missal, *De Defectibus*:

'VII — Defect of intention: [The intention of consecrating is required. Therefore there is no consecration in the following cases:] when a priest does not intend to consecrate but only to make a pretence; when some hosts remain on the altar forgotten by the priest, or when some part of the wine or some host is hidden, since the priest intends to consecrate only what is on the corporal; when a priest has eleven hosts before him and intends to consecrate only ten, without determining which ten he means to consecrate. On the other hand, if he thinks there are ten, but intends to consecrate all that he has before him, then all will be consecrated. For that reason every priest should always have such an intention, namely the intention of consecrating all the hosts that have been placed on the corporal before him for consecration.

'If the priest thinks that he is holding one host but discovers after the Consecration that there were two hosts stuck together, he is to consume both when the time comes. If after receiving the Body and Blood, or even after the ablution, he finds other consecrated pieces, large or small, he is to consume them, because they belong to the same sacrifice. If, however, a whole consecrated host is left, he is to put it into the tabernacle with the others that are there; if this cannot be done, he is to consume it.

'It may be that the intention is not actual at the time of the Consecration because the priest lets his mind wander, yet is still virtual, since he has come to the altar intending to do what the Church does. In this case the Sacrament is valid. A priest should be careful, however, to make his intention actual also.

the Church does' which, in this case, is sacrificially to turn the entire substances of the bread and wine into those of the Body and Blood of Christ, made truly, really and substantially present with his soul and divinity under the remaining externals of bread and wine, for the salvation of the world. This intention would suffice. On the contrary, a priest who would wilfully withdraw his intention to consecrate while performing the ritual gestures and uttering the sacramental formulas would commit the grave sin of *simulatio in sacris*.[25] While such a risk is thankfully alien to most priests, it is a salutary warning to all of us. But our concern here is not about hypothetical deceivers. It is about fellow-priests who might involuntarily be led by defective circumstances into a hazy perception of their sacramental actuation when concelebrating.

2) A historical precedent: The hypothesis of a gradual shift from sacramental to ceremonial concelebration would not be unprecedented (nor culpable *per se*), as the case of the ordination Mass illustrates. In the thirteenth century, in his *Summa Theologiae*, St Thomas Aquinas describes as *sacramental* the concelebration of Holy Mass by the new priest during his ordination ceremony.[26] This would have been one of the rare occurrences of sacramental concelebration in medieval times. But the nature of this concelebration seems to have changed since St Thomas witnessed it. At ordinations in the Extraordinary Form of the Roman rite currently in force, and substantially identical to the Dominican rite

25 'Innocent XI condemned the proposition that instant and grave fear is a just cause for simulating the administration of the sacraments. From this it follows that not only formal simulation with the intention of deceiving others is wrong, as being a lie in action, but even material simulation of administering a sacrament, whereby the matter or the form of a sacrament is used without the making of the sacrament, is not justified by grave fear. The minister may not give an unconsecrated host to a sinner as communion, or fictitiously absolve a penitent even to avoid death. The reason is because by so doing he would abuse a holy rite, instituted by Christ, and thus be guilty of gross irreverence toward God. It is a less sin for a priest to celebrate unworthily than to pretend to say Mass and not consecrate.' Cf. *Manual of Moral Theology*, by Thomas Slater, S.J.; Book II, No. 40, (New York: Benziger Brothers, 1908).
26 Cf. IIIa, Q82, a2.

St Thomas would have known, various signs point towards a *ceremonial* concelebration rather than sacramental.

First of all, the priests just ordained do not stand near the altar during Consecration but remain on their knees at a distance, generally on the lower sanctuary level, rather than upon the predella or upper step where the pontiff stands. Instead of reading with him from the altar missal, each newly ordained separately reads the prayers from a missal set on a free-standing low lectern. This posture precludes seeing the gifts on the *mensa* of the altar. Neither do they hold bread or wine at the consecration. Unlike modern concelebrants, they do not communicate themselves to the sacred host, but have a small host set on their tongue by the bishop, while kneeling like any other communicant. Furthermore, they do not drink the Precious Blood from the chalice. Towards the end of Holy Mass, the bishop admonishes them *not to offer Holy Mass until thoroughly trained by an expert priest* — which could suggest that they haven't just offered it. Finally, unlike concelebrants at sacramental concelebrations in ordinary occasions, the newly ordained do not receive a stipend for concelebrating their ordination Mass.

For want of an authoritative answer, one could legitimately question the sacramental nature of their concelebration. It looks rather like an ultimate rehearsal *in situ*, under the guidance of the ordaining bishop acting as chief tutor. If this is the case, the concelebration of the ordination Mass would have shifted indeed from sacramental[27] to ceremonial since the thirteenth century. Could a similar evolution have occurred, on some occasions, over the shorter period of the past fifty years in the Western Church? If this hypothesis were proven, a certain number of concelebrants would participate in Holy Mass without, however, offering it *in persona Christi*. The fruits derived would be genuine, but more akin to those stemming from the purposely *ceremonial* concelebration described earlier, still in use in the Extraordinary Form of the Roman rite and in Oriental rites. Any priest present at Holy Mass should of course know unambiguously (and let it be known)

27 According to St Thomas Aquinas' witness.

whether he means to transubstantiate or not. If he means to, the conditions offered must objectively allow transubstantiation to take place. The more a priest knows, believes in and reveres the objective reality of his priestly character and of the Eucharistic presence as stated by the Magisterium, the more he will seek clarity about the exact nature of his concelebration in any given circumstance, either sacramental, or ceremonial.

CONCLUSION

Priestly unity cannot be manifested except in relation to the Most Holy Sacrament of the altar. *Ceremonial* concelebration of Holy Mass has long been a way of fostering and expressing Eucharistic unity among clerics of both Western and Eastern Churches. It traditionally took place with and around the bishop. The priests present participated actively without transubstantiating with the bishop, but in a combined liturgical service with their fellow clerics of lesser ranks. Since the 1960s however, *sacramental* concelebration has been imposed in the West as the main expression of priestly unity. In many cases, sacramental concelebration is deemed the only necessary and sufficient sign of unity. This leads to fewer Holy Masses being offered, since one Mass occurs per concelebration rather than per concelebrant. One cannot be indifferent to this problem, if one remembers that the saving merits of Christ acquired on the cross will not bear fruit unless subsequently applied to the needs of souls. Since this application is supremely achieved at Holy Mass, diminishing without due cause the number of Holy Masses offered deprives souls of the graces they need. Consequently, Holy Mother Church reasonably recommends the multiplication of Holy Masses, which systematic sacramental concelebration hinders. Instead, the latter introduces risks to clergy and laity alike. With some perspective, one realises that sacramental concelebration is one option among various signs of sacramental unity. These signs were successfully used for nineteen centuries, up to the 1960s. Fundamentally, priests are in true communion when united in Eucharistic faith, reverent worship and rubrical loyalty. Dear fellow priests, let us pray for theological clarification on this important issue of concelebration, because of its bearing upon our priestly identity and upon our service to souls. Meanwhile, let us rejoice in the magisterial assurance that, *as often as this saving victim is offered up, so often is furthered the work of our redemption.*

7

Building The Bride

OLD AND NEW EVE

This chapter draws a parallel between the creation of Eve and the Eucharistic origin of the Church. In the Book of Genesis (2:23), God presents the newly created Eve to Adam just awakened from his sleep. The first Adam marvels: *This is bone of my bones and flesh of my flesh.* Such is the well-known first declaration of love from the first man to the first woman. This episode echoes another instance when the New Adam spoke similar words, having in mind the New Eve, his Church. The night he was betrayed, before he suffered, the Lord Jesus said: *This is my Body.... This is my Blood.* He uttered these sacred words while holding bread and wine, changing their substance into those of his own Body and Blood, truly separated on the Cross the following day. Let us explore the parallel between the creation of Eve of old in the Garden of Eden, and of the New Eve in the Upper Room and in the Garden of Golgotha.

Let us define who the New Eve is. This ancient title applies individually to the Blessed Virgin Mary and collectively to the Holy Catholic Church. In either case, the New Eve stands as the helpmate of Christ the New Adam. As a couple, the New Adam and the New Eve fulfil the redemption promised to Adam and Eve of old after their original sin in the Garden of Eden, when God told the serpent: *I will put enmities between thee and the woman, and thy seed and her seed: she shall crush thy head* (Gn 3:15). As man, the Lord Jesus Christ is literally 'the seed' of the Blessed Virgin Mary and as such, is her Son biologically. But this Man is also her God and Lord. Jesus and Mary are constantly united to give life to souls, but more visibly at Cana and Golgotha. They are Mother and Son according to the Incarnation, and also spiritual

Spouses according to the Redemption. Christ the New Adam is Head and Bridegroom of humanity redeemed. The spousal relationship between him and the Immaculate Virgin Mary is extended to the entire human race cleansed from sin, that is, the Church.

WHAT THE EARLY FATHERS WROTE

Among various Fathers of the Church such as St Irenaeus, St Ambrose and St Augustine, the martyr Methodius of Olympus[1] bears witness to this doctrine:

> The apostle [Paul] directly referred to Christ the words which had been spoken of Adam. For thus will it be most certainly agreed that the Church is formed out of his bones and flesh; and it was for this cause that the Word, leaving his Father in heaven, came down to be joined to his wife (Eph 5:31); and slept in the trance of His passion, and willingly suffered death for her, that he might present the Church to himself glorious and blameless, having cleansed her by the laver (Eph 5:26-27), for the receiving of the spiritual and blessed seed, which is sown by him who with whispers implants it in the depths of the mind; and is conceived and formed by the Church, as by a woman, so as to give birth and nourishment to virtue.

St Methodius goes on, now focusing on the production of the Church out of Christ in the Holy Sacrifice of the Mass:

> For in this way, too, the command, "Increase and multiply" (Gn 1:18), is duly fulfilled, the Church increasing daily in greatness and beauty and multitude, by the union and communion of the Word who now still comes down to us and falls into a trance by the memorial of his passion; for otherwise the Church could not

1   Also called Eubulius, who died c. 311.

conceive believers, and give them new birth by the laver
of regeneration, unless Christ, emptying himself for
their sake, that he might be contained by them, as I
said, through the recapitulation of his passion, should
die again, coming down from heaven, and being joined
to his wife, the Church, should provide for a certain
power being taken from his own side, so that all who
are built up in him should grow up, even those who
are born again by the laver, receiving of his bones and
of his flesh, that is, of his holiness and of his glory.[2]

WAS THE NEW EVE IN THE UPPER ROOM?

Was the New Eve, i.e. the Church, present at the Last Supper, in
the Upper Room? Not in a state of completion, the way Eve of old
stood in the Garden of Eden. On Maundy Thursday the New Eve was
present inchoatively as Christ, her divine Spouse, instituted the Holy
Eucharist and the sacred priesthood, ordaining the Twelve Apostles.
She was present in Christ's Eucharistic gifts, albeit in a nascent stage.
Why was it so? Because the Church grows from the Holy Eucharist.[3]
Holy Mass is the unbloody re-enactment of Christ's sacrifice on
the Cross. This unique sacrifice merited for all men salvation from
their sins, as a redeemed people. The Holy Sacrifice of the Mass
extends and applies to baptised people of all times and all places
the saving merits of Christ crucified. It channels his substance into
them through Eucharistic Communion, as his mystical Body, the
Church. The Church as the New Eve was fully present in the same
Upper Room though, on Pentecost fifty-three days later, when Christ
her divine Head insufflated her with her divine Soul, his Holy Spirit.

Standing at the foot of the Cross on Good Friday, St John bears
witness to the water and blood flowing from the side of Christ
opened by the soldier's lance. The Church always referred this

---

2   Cf. *Symposion* also known as *Banquet of the Ten Virgins*, Discourse
III, Chapter 8.

3   This is the title of Pope John Paul II's encyclical on the Holy Eucharist,
Ecclesia de Eucharistia, 17 April 2003.

issuing of blood and water to holy Baptism and the Holy Eucharist, her two most fundamental sacraments. In the Upper Room the evening before, then, the New Adam knew that his very side would imminently be opened according to God's will, for humanity redeemed to be shaped out of his sacrifice. When Christ consecrated bread and wine for the very first time, he had in mind all those who would welcome his redemption and be saved, once gathered into his Mystical Body, the Church. Indeed, the word 'church' means not only the definite group of the elect, but also their convocation — *ekklesia* in Greek.[4] The New Adam is the One who proclaimed this call to unity: *That they all may be one, as thou, Father, in me, and I in thee; that they also may be one in us* (Jn 17:21). He spoke these words on Maundy Thursday, the same evening when he instituted the Eucharistic sacrifice.

In the Garden of Eden, when Adam of old first praised his newly formed wife, he did not envisage suffering and sacrifice, but perfect bliss in natural complementarity. He did not know then that Eve would pluck the forbidden fruit and that he would, at her invitation, eat of the tree. On the other hand, when the New Adam offered himself for his bride the Church in the Upper Room, he knew that only his forthcoming sacrifice on the tree of the Cross in the Garden of Golgotha would redeem his beloved, finally born of him. The fruit he would share with her was to be his own flesh and blood, out of which she would be shaped anew. Thus, the first Eucharistic consecration on Maundy Thursday must be considered together with the Crucifixion on the following afternoon. They are two stages of one action, namely, the sacrificial re-creation of fallen humanity for its espousals with God the Son.

THIS IS BONE OF MY BONES

We can now look more in detail at the words spoken by the old Adam and the New One. Adam of old said: *This is bone of my bones and flesh of my flesh.* The New Adam said: *This is my body. . . . This*

---

4   Cf. *Catechism of the Council of Trent*, Creed, Article IX: 'The word *ecclesia* (church) means *a calling forth*.'

is . . . my blood. Thus, bone and body are uttered first, flesh and blood after. This expresses anatomical precedence, as the flesh needs the bones to be supported by them; just like the blood needs the body to run through. In both cases, a more important corporeal component (bone, body) is mentioned before a less important one (flesh, blood). It could be suggested that the hierarchical complementarity between bone and flesh on the one hand, and between body and blood on the other hand, prefigures or replicates that of the man in relation to the woman. Both are united within the same conjugal entity, as head to body according to St Paul's teaching: *Because the husband is the head of the wife, as Christ is the head of the church. He is the saviour of his body* (Eph 5:23). This relationship applies to the first human couple and to any husbands and wives. But it also applies to Christ in relation to his mystical Body, the Church.

In Hebrew the expressions 'bone of my bones' and 'flesh of my flesh' must be understood literally. They refer to the actual organic matter taken by God from Adam's body to build the body of Eve, his wife. 'Of' translates here the Hebraic preposition 'min' (in various contracted, prefixed forms). This preposition means 'from, out of.' So the translation 'flesh of my flesh' means 'flesh *from* my flesh.' But the same expressions are also used metaphorically in other biblical episodes, to express kinship, fellowship and citizenship. The metaphorical use of the expressions is derived from its literal use. As such, it stresses the ontological unity between the first human spouses, Adam and Eve. Applying this meaning to the words of consecration spoken by Christ on Maundy Thursday enhances the spousal intention of the New Adam. Yes, a bloody sacrifice was the means chosen by God's wisdom to restore harmony between fallen mankind and the Holy Trinity. But suffering was not to be the last word. The end was union fulfilled in a spousal embrace of grace, everlastingly.

Non Hebraic readers are likely to interpret 'bone of my bones' and 'flesh of my flesh' as a poetical emphasis. In that sense, the expression conveys the superlative quality of 'this' bone and 'this' flesh. An equivalent would be: 'These are my bone and flesh *par excellence*, or superlatively.' To speakers of European languages, this sounds similar[5] to the Hebraic expressions 'God of gods, and Lord of lords' (Dt 10:17), Virgin of virgins (a title of Our Lady in her litanies), holy of holies (the most sacred part of the sanctuary in the Temple of Jerusalem), servant of the servants of God (a title for the Sovereign Pontiff), *in saecula saeculorum* (forever and ever — literally: for centuries of centuries). Thus, Adam describes his newly formed wife as superlatively his because, unlike the animals, Eve shares his very nature.

In the New Testament, the New Adam insists similarly on the superlative quality of the bread he wants to feed us with, on behalf of his Father. In the *Our Father* indeed, Jesus uses a word occurring nowhere else in the Greek bible, not even in the Greek language in general: *epiousios* (επιούσιος), which can be translated as 'supersubstantial.' Commentators explain the choice of this word by Christ's intention to announce the Eucharistic Bread rather than ordinary bread. A Hebraic equivalent of *epiousios* could be 'bread of breads' (in Latin *panis panium*). We know that the Lord Jesus meant this 'bread of breads' to be his own Body, Blood, Soul and divinity, that is, the substance of his being to be shaped into his mystical Bride the Church as his God-given match. Thus, both Adams imagine a new way of expressing the unsurpassable excellence of their brides built out of their own substance.

GOD BUILT THE RIB INTO A WOMAN

God built the rib into a woman (Gn 2:22). Why does the sacred author use here the verb 'to build'? It belongs to the vocabulary of architecture, not of anatomy. 'To build' normally applies to material components, not to organic ones, or to living beings. The same word 'to build' occurs later on in Genesis for the building of the city and

---

5   Further to our mention above, the idiomatic Hebraic construction where A is in a genitive relationship to B, like 'king of kings,' is not the one used here, where instead 'min' indicates the origin. The Septuagint gives 'ἐκ' to translate 'from,' also indicating the origin. Although unsupported by grammar, we include the 'superlative' interpretation as secondary because it does not contradict the 'original' one but rests upon it inasmuch as Eve's literal origin from Adam is what makes her supremely dear to him.

tower of Babel, for Noah's ark and for building altar and cities. It is used figuratively for building up strength, character and family.

Our Lord uses the same verb to announce that he will build his Church upon Simon Peter: *Thou art Peter, and upon this rock I will build my church* (Mt 16:18). Later on, the Jews misquote the Saviour: *We heard Him say, "I will destroy this man-made temple, and in three days I will build another that is made without hands"* (Mk 14:58). But according to St John, Our Lord did not use the verb 'to build' but 'to raise': *Jesus answered, and said to them: "Destroy this temple, and in three days I will raise it up"* (Jn 2:19). To this the Jews answer quoting Our Lord (correctly this time), without understanding his use of the word 'to raise': *"This temple took forty-six years to build,"* the Jews replied, *"and You are going to raise it up in three days?"* (Jn 2:20). Jesus seems to apply to a building, the temple, the verb 'to raise' which is used in the Bible about human persons. Conversely, in Genesis, the verb 'to build' normally applied to buildings was used in reference to Eve, a human person. This confirms the correspondence, in God's revelation to men, between Eve as the old Adam's literal bride and the Church as the New Adam's mystical bride.

From this enquiry, we see that the first Eve is 'built' from Adam's rib into a woman, because the New Eve, the Church, will be built from the side of the New Adam. The architectural connotation of the verb 'to build' strikes as inaccurate in relation to Eve of Eden, but it proves beautifully fitting to the shaping of the New Eve, the Church, which is a spiritual structure. St John saw the mystical bride of Christ appear at an embryonic stage on Golgotha: *But one of the soldiers with a spear opened his side: and immediately there came out blood and water. And he that saw it hath given testimony* (Jn 19:34-35). The same witness rejoices when beholding the full stature of Christ's mystical bride at the end of time, as he describes in his Apocalypse: *And I John saw the holy city, the new Jerusalem, coming down out of heaven from God, prepared as a bride adorned for her husband* (Apoc. 21:2). Adam's rib is thus prophetically 'built' into a woman, announcing the Church to come, just as after the first sin, the woman's seed which will crush the head of the serpent prophetically refers to Christ.

THE EUCHARISTIC BUILDING OF THE BRIDE

Applied to the Eucharistic sacrifice, the building up of the New Eve, Christ's mystical bride, is expressed in the rite of consecration, and later on in the rite of the *commixio* or commingling. Let us look first at the rite of consecration. There, the successive consecrations of the bread turned into Christ's Body, then of the vine turned into Christ's Precious Blood, represent the separate components of the Church in the making. It is akin to reckoning what will be needed to complete the construction, as Our Lord Himself once advised: *For which of you having a mind to build a tower, doth not first sit down, and reckon the charges that are necessary, whether he have wherewithal to finish it* (Lk 14:28).[6] Second, let us consider the rite of commingling. Before the *Agnus Dei*, the priest drops a particle of the sacred Host into the Precious Blood, saying: *May this commingling and consecrating of the Body and Blood of Our Lord Jesus Christ avail us who receive it unto life everlasting. Amen.* This rite brings together the two Eucharistic species of bread and wine, after their separate consecrations. It can be seen as the assembling of the edifice, the building up of the Church, the New Eve, out of the substance of the New Adam. If even *the hairs of our head are all numbered* (Lk 12:7), to a much greater extent are the Holy Masses numbered in God's prescience. Each Eucharistic offering increases the figure of the Church, spiritually and materially, until the Last Judgement. The number of sacred hosts and the quantity of wine to be consecrated is known to God, as is the number of Holy Communions to be received. These are a supernatural equivalent of bricks and mortar as reckoned by the divine Builder of the Church.

6 The only mention of Jesus writing is when he was asked to judge the adulterous woman: *Jesus bowing himself down, wrote with his finger on the ground. When therefore they continued asking him, he lifted up himself and said to them: "He that is without sin among you, let him first cast a stone at her." And again stooping down, he wrote on the ground* (Jn 8:6–8). In the Old Testament, adultery is classically applied to the infidelity of God's Chosen People, forsaking his law. What the New Adam was writing on the ground, one may surmise, was his reckoning of the expense needed to cleanse his future bride the Church, building her as the mystical tower of David.

Every Holy Mass points to life everlasting as to the completion of the building of the Church. The New Adam, who is God the Son, is building his bride as a tower reconnecting fallen humanity with heaven. Like the tower in the short parable quoted above, its construction costs demand reckoning, but Christ will provide the materials, namely his own flesh and blood. Christ's tower and holy city will rise to heaven and will stand forever, unlike Babel of old, abandoned by its proud builders: *Come let us make brick, and bake them with fire. And they had brick instead of stones, and slime instead of mortar: And they said: Come, let us make a city and a tower, the top whereof may reach to heaven; and let us make our name famous before we be scattered abroad into all lands. And the Lord came down to see the city and the tower, which the children of Adam were building.... And so the Lord scattered them from that place into all lands, and they ceased to build the city* (Gn 11:3-5; 11:8). Later on, the architectural metaphor applied by King Solomon to the bride in the *Song of Songs* is a prophecy of the Church, the mystical edifice built by the divine Bridegroom, Christ. We can hear him sing with delight the praises of his bride: *Thy neck, is as the tower of David, which is built with bulwarks: a thousand bucklers hang upon it, all the armour of valiant men* (Cant 4:4).

A DOOR FOR THE BRIDE

Whether it is a city, a house or a tower, an edifice must have a gate or a door. The same Hebrew verb 'to close' is used in Genesis for the door on the side of Noah's ark, closed by God after Noah has got inside with all the animals (Gn 7:16) and, five chapters earlier, for Adam's side closed by God after his rib has been built into the woman (Gn 2:21). In his commentary on St John's Gospel, St Augustine extends the parallel to the opening of the side of Jesus' dead body hanging on the cross:

'One of the soldiers with a spear laid open His side, and immediately came there out blood and water.' A suggestive word was made use of by the evangelist, in not saying pierced, or wounded his side, or anything

else, but opened; that thereby, in a sense, the gate of life
might be thrown open, from whence have flowed forth
the sacraments of the Church, without which there is
no entrance to the life which is the true life. That blood
was shed for the remission of sins; that water it is that
makes up the health-giving cup, and supplies at once
the laver of baptism and water for drinking. This was
announced beforehand, when Noah was commanded
to make a door in the side of the ark, whereby the
animals might enter which were not destined to perish
in the flood, and by which the Church was prefigured.
Because of this, the first woman was formed from the
side of the man when asleep, and was called Life, and
the mother of all living. Truly it pointed to a great good,
prior to the great evil of the transgression (in the guise
of one thus lying asleep). This second Adam bowed his
head and fell asleep on the cross, that a spouse might
be formed for him from that which flowed from the
sleeper's side. O death, whereby the dead are raised
anew to life! What can be purer than such blood? What
more health-giving than such a wound?

The side of the New Adam was never closed again, even after
his Resurrection, as we recall from Our Lord's invitation to St
Thomas incredulous: *Bring hither the hand and put it into my
side* (Jn 20:27). Further, we know that even after his Ascension
into Heaven, Christ as High Priest continues to intercede for us,
showing to God the Father his stigmata as titles for our salvation.
However, the side of the New Adam is closed in the persons of his
priests, whose chests are normally unscathed, during or outside of
Mass. A well-known exception is St Pio of Pietrelcina who, as a
priest, bore the visible stigmata of Christ until two days before his
death. Priests utter the sacred words of consecration at Holy Mass
in the Person of Christ the divine Bridegroom. They lend their
humanity to the New Adam to build further his mystical bride the
Church. Each priest celebrant should wonder at his unwounded

side. He should remember that under his unmarked skin, at least his heart should be pierced with love for God and men, after the Sacred Heart of Christ, his Model. Each priest should give thanks for the honour done him of bringing forth the New Adam's bride. The mouth of the priest when speaking the words of consecration expresses and produces the New Eve. In the 'sleep' of his sacrificial death on the cross, the New Adam could not speak when his side was opened by the lance; but every time his priests utter his words of the Last Supper: *This is my body... my blood*—we can hear him exclaim as once in Eden Adam of old: *This is bone of my bones and flesh of my flesh*. At the Eucharistic consecration in particular, the priest shares in the spousal love and power of the divine Bridegroom, entirely spent for his beloved bride the Church. Celibacy is undoubtedly the most eloquent sign of this identification of the priest celebrant to Christ the Spouse. If the priest is already married, then abstinence allows him to act more faithfully in the Person of Christ, the Virgin Spouse of Holy Church and souls. The priest opens his mouth at Consecration as the ministerial door for the bride to come forth: *This is my body... my blood*.

NAMING THE BRIDE

Both the old Adam and the New Adam Our Lord say *This is...* when defining their helpmate just shaped. In the Garden of Eden, looking at Eve for the first time, Adam says, '*This is* bone of my bones and flesh of my flesh.' In the Upper Room on Maundy Thursday, beholding bread and wine in his hands, Our Lord says '*This is* my body... my blood,' thus turning matter into the elements constitutive of the Church, his mystical bride. But the first Adam was only a man, unlike Our Lord who is also God. Consequently Adam did not create Eve, whereas Our Lord did bring the Church into existence, a process initiated with Eucharistic transubstantiation.

Adam also enjoyed a state of innocence before his sin, which made him more like Our Lord than we who are born after the sin. Thus, Adam spoke without error or deceit when naming his bride, but with truth, as dictated by his original integrity. Furthermore, God presented the woman to Adam precisely for him to name her: *The Lord God ... brought [the animals] to Adam to see what he would call them: for whatsoever Adam called any living creature the same is its name.... And the Lord God built the rib which he took from Adam into a woman: and brought her to Adam. And Adam said...* (Gn 2:19, 22). From this we understand that naming the woman is Adam's cultic praise to God for her creation, in which the splendour of its Maker is displayed. Without any hint of arbitrariness or imprecision, Adam's intellect still unclouded by sin shows him the very essence of this latest of creatures and, after having given a name to all animals, he declares *'She shall be called woman, because she was taken out of man.'*

Strikingly, Our Blessed Lord also addresses His Holy Mother as 'Woman' when about to die on the cross: *When Jesus therefore had seen his mother and the disciple standing whom he loved, he saith to his mother: Woman, behold thy son* (Jn 19:26). This occurs at the very end of his earthly life. He had used the same noun to address Our Lady at the very beginning of his public life, before performing his first miracle at Cana: *And the wine failing, the mother of Jesus saith to him: They have no wine. And Jesus saith to her: Woman, what is that to me and to thee? My hour is not yet come* (Jn 2:3-4). Thus, Our Lady is called Woman in reference to the Hour of the Sacrifice, when the precious blood of her Son, prefigured in the miraculous wine of Cana, will be poured out to found the Church. Our Lord says 'Woman' to other females than his mother, but the context of the Crucifixion, *'where there was a garden'* (Jn 19:41) in which the Cross stood as the new Tree of life, calls for the parallel with the Garden of Eden.

Adam later on specifies the naming of the woman: *And Adam called the name of his wife Eve: because she was the mother of all the living* (Gn 3:20). In Hebrew, 'Eve' literally means 'life-giver.' Indeed, the entire human race descends from Eve's progeny; not without suffering, according to God's judgement: *'in sorrow shalt thou bring forth children* (Genesis 3:16). Similarly, the New Adam Our Lord also specifies the name of the one he had just called 'Woman.' *After that, he saith to the disciple: "Behold thy mother"* (John 19:27). Truly, the Virgin Mary becomes through grace the Mother of all the elect, starting with St John. Notably then, Adam of old and the New Adam name their helpmate 'Woman' first, and soon after 'Mother.' While 'Woman' refers to Adam (old and New alike) as his God-given associate, 'Eve-Mother' refers to the children to be born to them; physically for Adam and Eve, spiritually for Our Lord and the Blessed Virgin Mary. In this case, the Sorrowful Mother stands as the embodiment of the entire Church, the Mystical bride of her Son. St John the Evangelist, the same first spiritual child of the Holy Mother, confirms this interpretation in his Apocalypse, Chapter 12, where the mysterious 'Woman' giving birth in pangs and escaping the infernal dragon refers both to Our Lady and to Holy Mother Church: *She was pregnant and cried out with pain because she was about to give birth. . . . Then the dragon was very angry with the woman. It went away to make war against all her other children. Her children are those who obey God's commands and have the truth that Jesus taught* (Apoc. 12:2,17).

We have drawn a parallel between the creation of Eve and the Eucharistic origin of the Church. This was based on the fact that the expression 'New Eve' refers individually to Our Blessed Lady and collectively to the Church, Christ's Mystical Body. Reading the words of the Eucharistic consecration at Holy Mass in the light of Adam's naming of Eve in Genesis enhances the spousal purpose of Christ's sacrifice. Christ, the New Adam, gave up his life to cleanse humankind, gathering all the elect as one spiritual entity, his bride the Church. This was formally achieved on Mount Golgotha when Christ died for our sins. But it was begun the night before, when in the Upper Room he offered his Body and Blood as the elements of the nascent Church. The shaping of the bride, the Church, is furthered every time priests offer the Holy Sacrifice of the Mass, acting in the Person of Christ.

The words used by the inspired author of the Book of Genesis to describe Adam's bride find their full meaning when applied to Christ's bride as through the lips of the New Adam. This occurs at Holy Mass. Eve was built by God as an individual bride, to become a mother according to biological life. The Church, typified by the Virgin Mary, is built by God as a mystical bride, and as a Mother according to supernatural life. Both brides literally come out of their husbands' substance, soon to foster life. Adam's love for Eve was ruined alas, through sharing in the sin of his bride. But Christ's love, the New Adam's, raises fallen humanity as his immaculate bride.

The words of Eucharistic Consecration at Holy Mass express the spousal love of Christ for humanity redeemed. These words are more powerful than those spoken in praise of Eve by the first Adam: *This is bone of my bones and flesh of my flesh.* In fulfilment of that prophetic song of love once uttered in Genesis, it is the honour of priests to speak the sacred words *This is my Body... my Blood,* lending their mouths to Christ as the ministerial doors through which the Church comes forth *as a bride adorned for her husband* (Apoc. 21:2).

8

Consecrated to God, Body and Soul[1]

THE TOTAL CONSECRATION TO GOD UPON which we reflect in this last chapter is shared by priests with religious of either sex. Priests draw encouragement from the example of religious. Secular priests in particular can easily be burdened by worldly concerns inherent to their service in the midst of the world. They are prompted to surrender themselves more radically and trustingly to Christ when encountering men and women religious whose solemn vows commit them more formally to poverty, chastity and obedience. Together, priests and religious offer to the world the salutary spectacle of a definitive and joyful gift of self to Christ, the Creator and Saviour of all men. Our reflections are also meant as a priestly tribute to religious; as a reminder to the laity in general of the honour owed to the religious state after the priestly one; and hopefully as an incentive for young people to consecrate themselves body and soul to God, in the religious or the priestly state. Lastly, while our examples focus on England, the trend described and the remedies suggested apply to other countries as well.

Better is one day in Thy courts above thousands. How lovely are thy tabernacles, O Lord of hosts! my soul longeth and fainteth for the courts of the Lord. This Introit[2] expresses the desire of our souls to spend our lives closer to God; actually to dwell in God's house as an anticipation of the blessed dwelling promised to us in God's celestial courts if we die in his grace.

This is why some Catholics will come to church every day. They do well. Even outside of Holy Mass, they will enter a Catholic church daily and pray to God truly present there. Other Catholics

1   This article was first published in *Dowry* No. 43, Autumn 2019.
2   Introit for Mass on the 14th Sunday after Pentecost, quoting Psalm 83:11.

want more. They want more than simply observing God's commandments. They choose to embrace God's *counsels* as well. They
want to spend their entire lives in close proximity to God's dwelling.
They withdraw from the secular world and organise their lives
together as religious communities. Their lives focus on prayer, religious study, penance and works of charity.

They want to give God every possible space in their hearts, in
their days and nights. To that end, they renounce earthly possessions through the vow of poverty. They give up the goods of
marriage and family bonds through the vow of chastity. Lastly,
through the vow of obedience, they offer up to God their own
will, as a beautiful sacrifice so as to follow the will of God in all
things through the legitimate will of their superiors.

Such is the religious state. It is a blessing for those called to it.
But it is also a blessing for those who witness it. Why is this so?

The religious state is a blessing for all, because it sets a higher
standard of perfection. It encourages all in the world to aspire to
a closer union with God while on earth, so as to enjoy it forever
in heaven. Since our human nature is fallen we constantly lean
towards the easier options, to the peril of our souls. This soon leads
us to venial sins and ultimately to mortal sins. On the other hand,
the presence of religious men and women near us demonstrates to
us that one can be blessedly fulfilled in poverty, chastity and obedience. Religious life manifests spiritual freedom on our doorstep.
And we all crave spiritual freedom. Contemplative religious also
pray for their fellow-Catholics in the world and welcome visitors
in their retreat centres, providing much-needed havens of silence
and prayer. Apostolic religious contribute actively to evangelisation
as mobile and flexible missionaries who can be deployed at short
notice to serve the needs of a given parish or diocese.

DISCERNMENT

Secular clerics must be even holier. What of priests who are not
in monastic life, one may ask? Are they dispensed from following
the three evangelical counsels of poverty, chastity and obedience?
On the contrary, even without taking the three vows of poverty,

chastity and obedience as religious do, secular clerics have an even greater obligation than religious to strive for perfection, as the Common Doctor of the Church teaches:

> Greater interior sanctity is needed for that very noble ministry in which Christ Himself is served in the sacrament of the altar, than is needed for the religious state. . . . Thus a cleric in sacred orders would, other things being equal, sin more grievously if he should do anything against sanctity than a religious who is not in sacred orders, although the lay religious is bound to regular observances to which those in sacred orders are not bound.[3]

This commitment of secular clerics to the evangelical counsels (whether in dioceses or in non religious communities such as the Priestly Fraternity of St Peter, the Oratorians, the Institute of Christ the King, the Good Shepherd Institute and others[4]) is manifested in the three prayers traditionally said when dressing every morning.[5] First, for the cassock: *O Lord, the portion of my inheritance and my chalice, You are He who will restore my inheritance to me. Amen.* This prayer expresses the cleric's dying to worldly possessions, for the sake of gaining Christ and being granted access to the Father's eternal kingdom. Indeed, the black cassock can be

---

3 *Summa*, 2-2, Q184, a8.

4 These communities stand half way between religious and secular clergy. Unlike religious they don't take vows. But like them and unlike diocesan clergy, they embody a distinctive charism, abide by their own constitutions, draw inspiration from one or several founders, lead communal life, and wear a distinctive habit. They are called clerical societies of apostolic life and are placed under the authority of the Holy See as to their internal life and charism, and under the local bishop as to their ministry in his diocese in accordance with their charism.

5 This point was mentioned in a previous chapter, but we repeat it here because it is a fitting reminder of the radical surrender expected of secular clergy, not only of religious. If already well informed of this truth, the reader may skip this paragraph.

seen as a shroud separating the man of God from earthly goods. Second, when putting on the collar, the cleric prays: *Set me under your sweet yoke, O Lord, and that of Mary your Mother.* This prayer asks for the virtue of obedience. The submission of the will is joyful and fruitful when intended to conform to the will of the Sovereign High Priest Jesus Christ and of his Immaculate Mother. This surrender will bear the fruit of humility and meekness, according to Christ the High Priest who taught: *Take up my yoke upon you, and learn of me, because I am meek and humble of heart . . . For my yoke is sweet and my burden light.* Third, when tying the cincture around his waist, the cleric says: *Gird me, O Lord, with the cincture of purity, and quench in my heart the fire of concupiscence, that the virtue of continence and chastity may abide in me.* We can admire the wisdom of Holy Mother Church, no doubt speaking for Our Lady herself, who knows well how necessary the virtue of chastity is for those who are to imitate the virginal Saviour.

Saving one's soul for heaven. Let us summarize our human condition. Configuration to Christ is necessary for salvation. Life in heaven is the real life, while life on earth prepares for it. Thus, we must organise our life on earth as an anticipation of heaven, free from the allurements of created goods. This is best secured through the three evangelical counsels of poverty, chastity and obedience. Christ practised them; religious orders implement them in various ways, whether contemplative or apostolic.

The holy Council of Trent warns that, *If any one saith, that the marriage state is to be placed above the state of virginity, or of celibacy, and that it is not better and more blessed to remain in virginity, or in celibacy, than to be united in matrimony; let him be anathema.*[6] Similarly, St Ignatius Loyola affirms that, *We must praise highly religious life, virginity, and continency; and matrimony ought not be praised as much as any of these.*[7] Certainly, marriage and family life

---

6 *Decree on the Sacrament of Matrimony,* Canon 10, on November 11, 1563. The references provided (Matt. 19:11; 1 Cor 7:25, 38, 40) show that the chastity envisaged here is not a transient resolution but a definitive commitment for the sake of the Kingdom.

7 *Rules for Thinking with the Church,* #4.

are excellent things, willed and blessed by God. In our day and age, the married state requires heroic virtues to be lived in perfection. Thank God for the courageous spouses and parents who give us such an example of fidelity and dedication. Matrimony and religious life (and the sacred priesthood) are not in competition with each other, but mutually beneficial. Together they flourish — or deteriorate. But religious life is a more radical surrender to God. It is like stepping disencumbered into eternity even before judgement. When we die, we will bring nothing with us but our good works and our merits. We will have nothing to present God with but his very grace, inasmuch as we will have welcomed it while on earth.

God calls no one to religious life as an escape from the hardships of marriage or factory or office work. Cloisters are not places for self-seekers. Cowls do not fit cowards. But a sober awareness of one's limitations combined with a painful experience of the seductiveness of modern society makes religious life a wise option. Fallen men and women are more likely to save their immortal souls in a community mandated by the Church for that explicit purpose. If such was the case in the bygone days of Christendom, how much more advantageous is religious life in our times of institutionalised vice and of state-of-the-art temptations!

How many lonely young men, sitting on their beds late at night, wish they had the courage not to visit certain websites on their cell phones. . . . Let these youngsters run to the cloisters instead, where their cells will be computer-free but crucifix-fitted, and where in a communal room the Internet will be used only, if at all, to order new candles and incense, or to answer prayer requests left on the community's website.

How many young women, weary of hoping for a trustworthy partner, will reluctantly slip in their handbag the pills they should never have bought in the first place on their way to that party, feeling that 'there seems to be no other way to get a man's attention'? Let them fly to a good convent instead. There, their faces surrounded by a comely wimple and veil, their hearts supported through sisterly friendship and enthused with holy purity, they will strive under the constant protection of the manliest of friends, the Lord Jesus, for whom every trusting soul is unique: *One is my dove, my perfect one* (Cant 6:8).

Weighing pros and cons. What if one fails though? What if one enters a religious community and sooner or later leaves it? Will it not be a waste of time? Will not people in the world laugh at such misfits, who thought themselves holier until, having hit the ceiling of their lofty dreams, they come down to earthly reality?

These concerns are valid. Prudence is needed, especially as regards the completion of studies before applying to a novitiate — if a genuinely Catholic university chaplaincy is available.[8] The advice of parents must be also considered out of the piety owed to them. However, parents have a duty to support vocations to consecrated life among their children and should welcome it as a grace from God for their entire family. If a child is the *only* support left on earth to his parents in their old age or disability, then the care of them takes precedence, and answering the call must be postponed as long as necessary. Furthermore, acquiring some life experience is useful in answering the call with less naivety and, once professed, to be protected against regrets born of an idealised perception of life in the world.

On the other hand, a religious calling (or a call to the priesthood) is a grace from God, both precious and fragile. Using the arguments listed above as excuses to cover up one's selfishness, ambition or cowardice could be gravely sinful. In addition, our fallen condition and the persuasive malice of modern society must be countered through a greater trust and generosity when considering a possible call. As for being mocked as misfits: the author personally knows of several men and women who left their communities while still in formation, and who are now fulfilled as spouses and parents, while lending their spiritual experience

---

8   The law of the Catholic Church stipulates that only *priests* (not even deacons) can be appointed (hence also called) chaplains: 'A chaplain is a priest to whom is entrusted in a stable manner the pastoral care, at least in part, of some community or particular group of the Christian faithful' (Can. 564). Non-priests appointed in a Catholic chaplaincy may be called assistants to the Chaplain.

to contribute actively to the life of their local parish or diocese. Provided they left for the right reasons, the discernment stage in their lives will have been an enrichment benefitting them and the wider Church. On the opposite side, one cannot *try* marriage, since the commitment lasts as long as one's spouse lives. People in the world can join third-orders whereby they share in the spirituality and in some privileges of religious orders as tertiaries or oblates.[9] This option can benefit those who find that they must remain in the world *after* having completed due discernment.

Assuredly, a traditional Catholic view is that each and every adolescent and young adult should earnestly and over a period of at least several months ponder before God with the help of a trusted priest whether they should enter Holy Orders or religious life. The freer from sentimental attachment one is at the time of discernment (and from vice even more so), the more reliably one will interpret God's response.

Some of the bitter consequences of the current sexual abuse crisis might have a cleansing effect by God's permission. One of them is fewer candidates wrongly applying for the sake of prestige and status. On the contrary, becoming a religious or a priest nowadays supposes that one will bear some of the opprobrium incurred by other consecrated people for their crimes. This is not without redemptive merit, after the example of the Saviour who, although innocent, was reviled and died for the sins of all men. However, those in civil society who truly thirst after justice will not despise a priest or religious for the sake of his habit, but rather will expect him or her to be faithful to the worthy purpose of his or her consecrated state.

---

9 Third-orders are associations attached to religious orders, providing people in the world with a certain sharing in the spiritual benefits of the religious order. Communities whose members do not take the three vows are not religious in a canonical sense, neither are the associations of faithful attached to them. However, joining such associations is very beneficial spiritually, e.g. the Confraternity of Saint Peter, whose 7,000 members worldwide pray daily for priestly vocations and ministry: www.fssp.org/en/help-us/confraternity-of-saint-peter/.

HISTORICAL PERSPECTIVE

Where to apply? How to answer a call to religious life in post-Christian Britain though, since most religious orders are in catastrophic decline, with few remaining members below seventy years of age? Sadly, this is part of the crisis which has been affecting the Church over the past sixty years. There are much fewer monasteries and convents than in the 1950s. Every month, some close down. Their handsome structures and spacious grounds, funded in ages of faith with the widow's mite, now make attractive spa-hotels, while some of the few young religious orders often lack adequate facilities. The vast amounts of money generated by the sale of these religious buildings to developers is immediately spent to cover the cost of healthcare for the elderly members of the community (often the majority); or even to pay the huge fines incurred by those convicted of crimes. The buildings still in religious use have often very few monks or sisters left, most of whom are generally near retiring age. How did it come to this?

All orders have fallen victim of the *aggiornamento* which, sixty years ago, was sold to the Bride of Christ as a rejuvenating unguent. The famous works of fiction by Anglican clergymen Jonathan Swift and Charles Dodgson (aka Lewis Carroll) can help us illustrate this spiritual metamorphosis. From the 1960s onward, many a religious sister felt as if having swallowed *Alice in Wonderland*'s cake with the tag '*Eat Me*'. We can picture a hypothetical 'Abbess Alice' subsequently growing out of proportion with her religious environment. Like Carroll's heroine, she suddenly feels constrained by the rule, the cloister and customs of her order as if they had shrunk around her soul. The change in her habit expresses this, as its sleeves withdraw from knuckles to elbows, its hem from heels to below knee and its veil from shoulders to nape; until civilian clothes replace it entirely. This quick evolution simultaneously affects her imaginary counterpart 'Prior Gulliver' whom we now envisage waking up in his cell one morning as Swift's character in Lilliput, strongly tied down with invisible strings, that is, the religious observances which in his eyes modernity turns into contemptible hindrances. As in Swift's tale, 'Prior Gulliver' eventually manages to break his bonds, emerging a 'free' man. He ends up either deserting his monastery or 'modernising' it, that is, pruning and purging the structure of his monastic life from its 'medieval accretions.'

Many saintly founders of once-flourishing communities would today have difficulty recognising the constitutions, habit, horarium, liturgy, enclosure, diet and curriculum they had prescribed through a charism of the Holy Ghost, with the Holy See's subsequent approval. If the same founders knocked at the door, not all their sons and daughters would recognise, welcome and follow them. Here in Britain, religious life was nearly wiped out first by the Saxons, later by the Danes, then by the Protestants. But this time, we did it to ourselves. We thought we knew better how to stay alive and even how to grow: instead, oblivious of the treasures we discarded, now we are dying.

White martyrdom. Over the past decades, while scores of thousands of contemplative and apostolic religious were leaving their monasteries and convents, many others stayed on with heroic obedience and hope. Noticing the painful contradictions with their founders' intuitions and the approved customs of their orders, these religious either doubted or opposed the new ways, but remained in any case. Why did they not leave? Because they knew that religious life is essential to the Church and because they trusted that God would make them bear fruit according to his holy will. Thus, they were stripped of the cherished traditions which had attracted them in the first place to this order or that convent, and which had shaped their calling and guided their response for the love of God and neighbour.

Not a few underwent this process in imitation of the Saviour's stripping of his garments. According to tradition, Our Lady had spun with her virginal hands the seamless tunic for her Son Jesus. After Our Lord's example, these religious found themselves exposed to the contempt of the world and soon nailed to the Cross in spirit. In communities whose *raison d'être* was divine worship, they had to undergo the impoverishment of the liturgy, quickly disfigured through trite innovations or even disgraceful improvisations. Most religious priests stopped offering individually the Holy Sacrifice of

the Mass, while non-priests were bullied through liturgical anar-
chy. Enclosed nuns in particular were at the mercy of whichever
celebrant was assigned to them, and were often subjected to his
liturgical abuses and doctrinal whims — a bitter paradox for an age
claiming to free Catholic women from 'clerical oppression.' Simultaneously, within orders whose charism was intellectual more than
liturgical, orthodox members were subjected to the no less painful
process of doctrinal deformation. Those who would not promote
modern ambiguities and errors were intimidated, ridiculed, pushed
aside, and forbidden to publish and to teach.

As the years went by, these pitiable religious (whether contemplative or apostolic) must have offered up their silent and unnoticed
sufferings for the welfare of the Church and the glory of God.
Many died of sadness, heartbroken, clinging in bitter desolation
to the promise they had once received as novices, long before,
when the One calling them to the religious state had whispered
to their young souls: *Never will I abandon you.* Please God, as
they closed their weary eyes they heard his voice again: *Well done,
good and faithful servant . . . enter thou into the joy of thy Lord*
(Mt 25:20) — from him whose Sacred Heart was also pierced for
the sins of all men. They were in good company if they suffered
with Our Lady's Immaculate Heart, with her whose white martyrdom co-redeemed the world. Secular clergy who offered up
similar trials endured in the context of their seminaries, parishes,
deaneries and dioceses are included in our gratitude. The sacrifices
of so many of these religious, nuns, seminarians, priests and even
bishops constitute a treasury of merits stored up in God's mercy
for the new generation to use.

The traditional few. In various countries from the 1970s onwards,
notably in France, other religious were inspired to found distinct
communities where the Church's time-tested traditions would be
upheld. To them as well the younger generations are indebted. With
patience, humility and perseverance, they demonstrated that the
Roman traditions could still be followed in communion with the
Church and for the benefit of souls. However, such communities
are as yet comparatively few. Thus, if one wishes to be formed

traditionally, and worship according to the traditional Roman liturgy in full canonical communion with the Church, the options are even fewer in this country. Those who like to have *habitually* the traditional liturgy can apply for the Marian Franciscan Friars and Sisters in Gosport, the Institute of Christ the King (for French-speakers), or the Benedictines of Silverstream Priory in Ireland. Men who want *simply* the traditional Latin liturgy can join the Sons of the Most Holy Redeemer in Scotland, or the Priestly Fraternity of St Peter (candidates for both communities are formed at the same English-speaking seminary in Denton, Nebraska).[10] Women can join a couple of traditional Carmels-in-formation in Great-Britain and several established ones in America. Less than three hours east from London outside Saint-Omer, the dying Benedictine abbey of St Paul-de-Wisques was saved from closure six years ago when traditional monks from Fontgombault took it over.[11] Could not this option be tried in England before it is too late for our dear Benedictine monasteries?

This gives us hope, but it still is insufficient, especially to satisfy *apostolic* vocations. What if a traditionally-minded Catholic in Britain aspires to join a teaching or nursing order such as the Salesians or the Daughters of Charity of Saint-Vincent-de-Paul, or a preaching one such as the Jesuits and the Dominicans? Over the years, we have also encountered a certain number of young men who were not called by God to become priests but who would have thrived as lay brothers if only that option had existed at the

10   French-speaking men can also apply for the excellent St Vincent Ferrer Fraternity, near Solesmes in France, where the Dominican traditions are lived to the full (www.chemere.org). In France, the male and female Benedictines of Le Barroux, and of Fontgombault with its daughter-communities (e.g. Clear Creek, Oklahoma) have preserved or restored traditional monastic life, although using a version of the liturgical books posterior to what is known as the Extraordinary Form of the Roman rite. In America, young women can visit the Benedictines of Mary in Gower, Missouri (benedictinesofmary. org) or the various traditional Carmels. This list is obviously not exhaustive. Across the Western world, various small new foundations deserve attention, prayer and funding.

11   Cf. *Dowry* No. 21, Spring 2014.

time. It was suppressed in most religious communities since the 1970s through a misguided sense of equality claiming that 'all had to be priests' or choir nuns. In effect, such upgrading denied the distinctiveness of a lay religious vocation. Paradoxically, this 'democratic' change prohibited religious life for all such young men (and women). They live the best they can while remaining in the world, although deprived of the specific frame of sanctification which they aspired to. This is unfair to them and detrimental to society. Had they been allowed to become consecrated brothers or sisters with that distinctive status, they would no doubt have grown into great spiritual assets to their communities and to the Church, as the earlier history of religious communities amply demonstrates.

THE TIME TO FOUND HAS COME

Such a lack of options, compared with the needs of a Catholic population under growing ideological pressure, suggests a possibility that can no longer be ruled out. Namely, the new generation may be called to found its own orders, or re-found or import some. Extreme caution is needed here because of pride, rashness, inexperience and illusions. God is the one who calls to religious life, and also the one who can raise founders and foundresses in a given time and country. But when devout Catholics look at the urgent need, it is timely for them to beg God for a revival of religious life here in Britain as well as in all our formerly Christian countries, like America; and even in places where Catholicism has so far been marginal. It is inspiring to learn the history of religious expansion in our country. It is pious to ask God that he may deign to make use of someone, however wanting in skills and experience, to help restore religious life throughout the land.

Walk in their footsteps. This will not sound like wishful thinking if one considers historical precedents in the life of the Church in this country:

• In 305, the young Protomartyr of England St Alban gave up his life to allow a missionary priest to continue the work of evangelisation.

- In 563, St Columba of Ireland founded a monastery on the western Scottish island of Iona.
- The Roman monk St Augustine of Canterbury landed in Kent in 597, and monasteries were established throughout England, notably in Lindisfarne with the saintly bishops and monks Aidan and Cuthbert.
- In 660, martyrdom-survivor St Winifred was abbess in Wales; in 664, St Hilda, abbess of the double monastery of Whitby, hosted a Synod decisive for English Catholicism; while in 673 St Etheldreda founded a double monastery at Ely.
- At the monastery of Jarrow in 731, St Bede the Venerable completed his *Ecclesiastical History of the English People*.
- English monks spread the faith far outside England, to mention here only the eighth century. St Willibrord (†739) and St Boniface (†754) evangelised The Netherland and Germany. In 782, the monk Alcuin of York—'the most learned man anywhere to be found'—became the main advisor to Emperor Charlemagne, fostering the Carolingian renaissance across Europe.
- Arrived in 1077 soon after the Conquest, the Order of Cluny was running twenty-four monasteries in England 58 years later.
- St Stephen Harding, in the twelfth century, co-founded the Cistercian order which spread fantastically; one hundred houses were founded within his lifetime, the first in England at Waverley, Surrey (1128). The Premonstratensians followed, with up to thirty houses across England.
- In 1181 St Hugh of Lincoln became Prior of the first Carthusian monastery founded in England.
- In 1184, the Knight Templars' headquarters was established in London; their round church still stands between Fleet Street and the River Thames.
- At Aylesford Carmelite Priory in Kent in 1251, St Simon Stock, General of his order, received the Brown Scapular from Our Lady.
- In the same thirteenth century, the mendicant orders founded by St Dominic and by St Francis started in England. Our streets and monuments still bear the names of Blackfriars (Dominicans), Whitefriars (Carmelites), Greyfriars (Franciscans) and Austin Friars (Augustinians).

And when all seemed lost. In the sixteenth century, once the Church had been wiped out from British lands through the tyranny of a lustful monarch supported by the greed of his entourage, everything seemed lost from a human perspective. And yet, God in his mercy called into action amazing initiatives of apostolic zeal, turning the blood of his religious martyrs into an ink of fire to write some of the most memorable pages of English history, sowing the seeds of the rebirth granted to the modern era.

• From the sixteenth century onwards, during the Protestant revolt and subsequent persecution of the Church, the newly founded Jesuits laboured for Christ across this land: notably Sts Edmund Campion, Robert Southwell, John Ogilvie; Fr John Gerard, and many other scholars, martyrs and educators. Older orders such as the Benedictines, the Carthusians and the Franciscans (and secular clergy) also gave many martyrs and confessors.

• In the nineteenth century, when the Catholic faith ceased to be persecuted, female religious communities appeared and multiplied, taking care of the children, of the poor, of the sick, and of the elderly. Let us list just a few of them: Institute of the Blessed Virgin Mary, Canonesses of the Holy Sepulchre, Franciscans Tertiaries, Poor Clares, Augustinians (Austin Dames), Carmelites, Cistercians, Visitation Nuns, Faithful Companions of Jesus, Ursulines of Jesus, Presentation Nuns, Sisters of Mercy, Good Shepherd Sisters, Sacred Heart Nuns, Providence (Rosminians), Notre Dame de Namur, Infant Jesus, Holy Child Jesus, Charity of St Paul, Franciscans of Immaculate Conception . . . and four times more!

• In the North West for instance, Bl. Dominic Barberi was assisted by the Servant of God Elizabeth Prout, later Mother Mary Joseph, the foundress of the Sisters of the Cross and Passion.

• Later in the nineteenth century, the Oratorians arrived. The Oratory was founded in Rome around 1552 by St Philip Neri, and imported into England by St John Henry Newman who founded the first Oratorian congregation in Birmingham in 1848, followed one year later by a second house in London; they are now also in Oxford, Manchester, York, Bournemouth, Cardiff. . . .

• For the Catholic education of boys, schools were founded by

Benedictine monks as well as by the Salesians of Don Bosco, De la Salle Brothers and others.

- In 1883, French Carthusians in exile founded the largest Charterhouse in the world in Parkminster, West Sussex. In 1903, the Tyburn Nuns arrived in London, also in exile from France, followed by many French religious.
- From 1904 until her death in 1942, Mother Mary of Jesus, a French Carmelite, née Madeleine Dupont, founded no less than thirty-three Carmels across England—more than St Teresa of Avila herself.
- In 1911, Saint Elisabeth Hesselblad founded in England a new branch of the Bridgettine order.
- More recently, convents of Mother Teresa's Missionaries of Charity spread, taking care of the homeless. (In London the Sisters readily attended the traditional Mass when offered for them.)
- Finally, in the year of the Lord 2020, with trembling and confident joy, *you* knocked at the door of...

Mystic Monks vs. Starbucks. A large framed map of religious houses across medieval Britain was once displayed on the wall of a retreat centre. Literally everywhere one could see the symbols for monasteries, abbeys, priories, nunneries, commanderies, etc. Most of them would have had attached to them a school, a hostelry for pilgrims or a hospital for the sick and poor. They were depicted on the map in various sizes and colours according to the religious order they belonged to: Cluniacs, Dominicans, Franciscans, Carmelites, Templars, Carthusians, Premonstratensians, etc. They shone as so many stars, an amazing constellation of powerhouses of consecration to God and of service to neighbours. How many of those still stand as houses of Catholic prayer and charity? What have we replaced them with? Supermarkets? Cinemas? A modern equivalent would be the map of coffee shops, spreading across the UK quicker than the Cistercian abbeys of old: light blue for Caffè Nero, dark blue for Costa, light green for Greggs, dark green for Pret A Manger, red for Wild Bin Café and pink for Starbucks Coffee. What we do not have yet in England is the Mystic Monk Coffee, a brand successfully started by the newly-founded traditional

Carmelite friars in Wyoming, USA. What now? We cannot revert to the medieval map of religious Britain. Can we catholicise the Starbucks Coffee map instead? Yes we can. By God's grace: reduce coffee; drop the bucks; reach for the stars.

Starting near you. Dear younger friends in particular, the holy traditions of the Church are time-tested means of sanctification and of configuration to Christ. Your generation has the wonderful privilege of widening the use of these holy traditions across the country and beyond. You are the ones who will found, re-found, restore religious life or innovate according to the dependable traditions, customs and virtues of Catholicism.

Through the mercy of God and the prayers of many, this may well have started already. As we write, three more young men from England and Northern Ireland have begun formation to the sacred priesthood at our international seminary in America. Over the past months, six young women in England, separately, shared with us their resolution to enter religious life very soon, three of whom have now begun their postulancy. Simultaneously, not far from us, three more young men started life in common to discern the will of God, while a fourth one does the same abroad under a priest's guidance. And surely there are many more young people elsewhere in Britain preparing for such wonderful commitments; and even more of them wishing for it, who only wait for a sign. Dear young friends, something is happening. Now is the time. Reach out. Do not remain isolated. Contact us. We will assist you. The time has come for the younger generation to enter the lists of consecrated life.

Now, in post-Christian Britain, now, we need *you* to revive the failing orders. Read their constitutions and history. Learn the life of their founders and ask for their intercession. Pray for their ageing members who meritoriously persevered during the on-going crisis. We are indebted to them.

New needs call for new orders. If it is God's will, as in earlier crises of the Church, you will import or start new orders. On the one hand, human nature remains fallen and does not change; neither does God's response, namely, grace. On the other hand, modernity brings new challenges, calling for inventive solutions. Now, with Catholic education hindered in many ways, we need consecrated men and women who will reach out to children and families and teach natural law and divine law. Now, when so many young adults are being undermined in their God-given sexual identity, we need consecrated celibates who will care tactfully for them. Now, with an ever-accelerating consumption and information frenzy, we need contemplatives offering to souls the balm of silence and stillness. Now, with abortion hailed as a right and baby parts at auction, we need new congregations trained specifically for pro-life work and for bio-ethical study. Now, with euthanasia prowling about the elderly and those gravely ill, and soon the disabled as once in eugenic Third Reich, we need new religious orders dedicated to medicine and nursing to protect their frailty. Now, with womanhood sullied through pornography, contraception and feminism, we need female religious embodying the Marian splendour of true womanhood, in fruitful consecration after Our Lady's example. Now, with shrinking parishes, ageing congregations and weary liturgies, we need expert clerics to display the sacred mysteries on a full liturgical scale to the glory of God and the edification of worshippers. Now, with Islam and aggressive secularism on the rise together, we need learned and fearless religious to preach redemption through Jesus the only Saviour, for the love of the triune God and the salvation of every soul.

Dear young friends, do not nibble at life in Christ: embrace it fully. Dive into grace. Enter the lists. For too long you have been hiding in the wood: now step onto the field. Become a monk. For too long you have sat on the fence: now fight for Christ and souls. Become a priest. For too long you have hunted short-lived fun: now invest all in everlasting joy. Become a nun.

Leave the world behind, to better lead it to Christ. Step into eternity, embracing Christ's own way of life: poor, chaste and obedient. Be passionate for God's honour and the salvation of the souls he redeemed through his Blood. In humble petition to God Almighty, call on the formidable power of intercession of the thousands of saintly British monks, friars, nuns, sisters and priests throughout the seventeen centuries of British Christianity! None of them was born a saint. Like you they felt inadequate to the task. But they trusted in God, like you should. Ask them. They will obtain for you metamorphoses more wondrous than those mentioned earlier in Swift and Carroll's fiction: by God's grace, sitting ducks will become soaring doves and fat calves will be turned into leaping deer: *As the hart panteth after the fountains of water; so my soul panteth after thee, O God!* (Ps 42:21).

Life is short and judgement nigh: begin today. *O God, better is one day in Thy courts above thousands. How lovely are thy tabernacles, O Lord of hosts! my soul longeth and fainteth for the courts of the Lord.* May we, secular clergy in particular, support your generous response through wise spiritual advice, through orthodox teaching, with pure hearts, through dignified liturgies and through our joyful and fruitful fidelity to our priestly calling. And may Our Lord and Our Lady, and the countless saints from Britain, from Ireland and from whichever country you live in, assist you in answering the call, now.

BIBLIOGRAPHY

ON THE PRIESTHOOD IN GENERAL

The Priest in Union with Christ, by Fr Reginal Garrigou-Lagrange OP

Christ: The Ideal of the Priest, by Bl. Columba Marmion OSB

The Priest is Not His Own, by Fulton Sheen

The Holy Eucharist-The World's Salvation, by Joseph de Sainte-Marie, Gracewing

ON RELIGIOUS LIFE IN ENGLAND *(among many other good books)*

The Saga of Citeaux, First Epoch: Three Religious Rebels: The Forefathers of the Trappists. Excellently dramatised by Fr. Mary Raymond Flanagan, O.C.S.O., this book illuminates the lives of St. Robert, St. Alberic and St. Stephen Harding, who taught the first Cistercians how to be "gallant to God" and make "no compromises."

Life of St Thomas à Becket, by Mrs Hope, London: Burns & Oates, 1868.

The Angel of Syon, the Life and Martyrdom of Bl. Richard Reynolds, Bridgettine Monk, by Dom Adam Hamilton OSB, Sands & Co, 1905.

John Gerard, Autobiography of an Elizabethan, translated by Philip Caraman, Family Publications, 2006 (cf. article in *Dowry* No 42).

The Last Abbot, by A. F. Webling, Edmund Ward, Leicester, 1944. A poignant dramatised narrative on the end of the great Abbey of St Edmunds in Bury Saint Edmunds under Henry VIII.

Edmund Campion: Jesuit and Martyr, by Evelyn Waugh, 1935.

A Benedictine Martyr in England, Dom John Roberts OSB, by Dom Bede Camm, OSB, London: Bliss, Sands & Co, 1897.

Memoirs of missionary priests, as well secular as regular, and of other Catholics, of both sexes, that have suffered death in England, on religious accounts, from the year of our Lord 1577, to 1684 / gathered, partly from the printed accounts of their lives and sufferings, published by contemporary authors, in divers languages, and partly from manuscript relations, kept in the archives and records of the English colleges and convents abroad, and oftentimes penned by eye-witnesses of their death, by Richard Challoner, London, 1742.

Ampleforth and Its Origins, edited by Abbot Justin McCann and Dom Columba Cary-Elwes, London: Burnes Oates & Washbourne, 1952.

The French Exiled Clergy in the British Isles after 1789, by Dom Dominic Aidan Bellenger OSB, Downside Abbey, Bath, England, 1986.

Fr Luigi Gentili and His Mission 1801–1848, by Denis Gwynn, Dublin, Clonmore and Reynolds, 1951. On the Rosminians in England.

Father Dominic Barberi, by Denis Gwynn, Kessinger Publishing, 2010. An inspiring account of the zeal for England of the saint who received John-Henry Newman into the Church.

A Job in Jeopardy, Elizabeth Prout, Foundress of the Sisters of the Cross & Passion, by Sister Barbara Sexton, C.P., Cross & Passion Communications, Salford, 2010. The perseverance of a young English convert who founded the female branch of the Passionists in England.

In the Silence of Mary. The Biography of the Life and Work of Mother Mary of Jesus, Notting Hill Carmel, London, 1964. The life of the French Carmelite who founded 33 Carmels throughout Britain between the years 1907 and 1938.

ABOUT THE AUTHOR

BORN IN 1971, FR ARMAND DE MALLERAY, FSSP
left France in 1994 after studying Literature for five years at the
Sorbonne in Paris. After teaching French at the Military Academy
in Budapest, he joined the Priestly Fraternity of St Peter in 1995 in
Bavaria, where he was ordained in 2001. He authored the *Art for Souls*
series of CD-ROMs presenting the Catholic faith through Christian
paintings by Georges de La Tour, Caravaggio, Rafael, Michelangelo
and Titian (each of the three volumes was granted official approval
by the President of the then-Pontifical Council for Culture). His first
priestly assignment was in London, Southwark Archdiocese. He served
in England since, apart from five years in Switzerland, then in an
administrative position at his Fraternity's headquarters. Since 2008, he
has been the editor of *Dowry*, the quarterly magazine of his Fraternity
in the UK & Ireland.

The book is based on the author's preaching experience, especially
to fellow clergy and seminarians. For a dozen years, Fr de Malleray
has preached fundamental retreats to clergy on themes such as *The
Year of Faith*, *The Year of Mercy*, *Our Lady and the Priest*, *The Prayers
of the Missal*, *The Priest and Martyrdom*, *The Priest and the Four Last
Things*, etc. Fr de Malleray also gave talks on the Holy Eucharist in
parishes during the International Eucharistic Congresses of Quebec
City (2008) and Dublin (2012), and further talks as a preparation
for the National Eucharistic Congress in Liverpool (7–9 September,
2018), as well as to Eucharistic ministers in the Portsmouth Diocese
(on Eucharistic fragments and concomitance). The author gathered
these Eucharistic reflections in the book *Ego Eimi: It is I — Falling in
Eucharistic Love*, published in 2018 by Lumen Fidei, Ireland, with a
Foreword by Bishop Athanasius Schneider.

Fr de Malleray has been chaplain to the international *Juventutem*
youth movement since its inception in 2004 (cf. www.juventutem.org),
and to its London group since 2015. The *Juventutem* logo is a monstrance and Eucharistic devotion holds pride of place in the movement.
With the *Juventutem* young adults, Fr de Malleray took part in the
World Youth Days of Cologne, Sydney, Madrid and Krakow. *Juventutem* worked hard to secure at World Youth Day official recognition

for the Extraordinary Form of the Roman rite. What was in 2005 in Cologne a sensational precedent has since become an expected and valued component of Word Youth Day.

By appointment from his superiors in the FSSP, since 2007 the author has been chaplain to the Confraternity of St Peter, a 7,000-strong international prayer network in support of priestly ministry and priestly vocations.

Since 2015, Fr de Malleray is the rector of St Mary's Shrine in Warrington, Liverpool Archdiocese, where he also oversees the apostolate of his Fraternity in England and promotes vocations to the priesthood.

Sometimes the language and concepts surrounding the Eucharistic Mystery can be difficult or impenetrable for many people. Fr Armand de Malleray has a gift in explaining traditional doctrine and practice without losing anything in depth or precision. In a lively, innovative and engaging style *'Ego Eimi - It is I'* passes on the timeless treasures of Traditional Catholic Faith and is a great service to the Church.

—FR MARCUS HOLDEN, author of the *Evangelium* catechetical series

This highly readable, informative, and edifying treatise on the Holy Eucharist will enrich the understanding and devotion of Catholics regardless of their prior knowledge of the subject: I recommend it wholeheartedly.

—DR JOSEPH SHAW, PhD, Oxf, Chairman of *The Latin Mass Society*

I heartily recommend this book to all.

—VERY REV JOHN M. BERG, FSSP, then-Superior General of the Priestly Fraternity of St Peter

Also available from
AROUCA PRESS

Meditations For Each Day
Antonio Cardinal Bacci

Integrity, Volume 2
The Second Year (January–June 1947)
Edited by Carol Robinson & Ed Willock

The Pearl of Great Price:
Pius VI & the Sack of Rome
Christian Browne

Liberalism:
A Critique of Its Basic
Principles and Various Forms
Louis Cardinal Billot, S.J.
(Newly translated by Thomas Storck)

Understanding Marriage & Family:
A Catholic Perspective
Sebastian Walshe, O. Praem.

CPSIA information can be obtained
at www.ICGtesting.com
Printed in the USA
FSHW011219150221
78590FS